History

2023

Volume LVII

Clark County History

Clark County History began publishing in 1960 as an annual project of the Fort Vancouver Historical Society. Publication was suspended temporarily in 2001 while the Fort Vancouver Historical Society restructured itself as the Clark County Historical Society and Museum. Publication resumed in 2004 under the auspices of the new organization.

Copies of this book and earlier editions are on sale at the Clark County Historical Museum 1511 Main Street, Vancouver WA 98660

CLARK COUNTY
HISTORICAL MUSEUM

Martin Middlewood, editor
Jan Anderson, assistant editor (on leave)
April Buzby, production
Masako Brachmann, cover

For permissions contact: outreach@cchmuseum.org

ISBN: 979-8-218-33365-2 (print)

Printed in the United States of America by Clark County Printing and Mailing Services, Vancouver, WA 98660

COVER PHOTOGRAPH
In a mock holdup, outlaws make off with a strongbox from the Chelatchie Prairie Railroad excursion train Aug. 19, 2023. (There were no known holdups of any Clark County trains.)

Photo by: Gregg Herrington

Contents

Articles

Looking Back

From the Staff

Caring for your museum's collection
Liza Schade 94

Bookmarks

Letter from the Executive Director

A s 2023 comes to a close, I'm heartened to see the amazing progress our museum has made over the last six decades. Furthermore, I'm excited to see what our future holds as we enter our 60th year of service for Clark County in 2024. In 1964, leaders of our community gathered together to create a space for residents of our county to explore their stories. As I've mentioned, those passionate individuals, and many in subsequent decades, laid the foundation for the success we see today. As a result, I looked back at the words of those who gathered to start the museum in 1964.

In the President's Report for 1964, Dr. John C. Brougher wrote of the excitement felt by all involved in this new endeavor. He exclaimed:

The year 1964 has been an eventful and rewarding one for the Fort Vancouver Historical Society [now known as the Clark County Historical Museum]...Beginning the last part of February a number of volunteer[s]...were at work every Thursday, and soon display cases were replacing the old library bookshelves. As time for the dedication drew near, some...worked every day in order to have the museum completed by the dedication date. I wish the others could have experienced the pleasure and enthusiasm manifested by these volunteers.

Looking back at this letter celebrating the beginning, I can clearly see the through lines of our story continued to this day. Dr. Brougher wrote next about the dedication of the museum team from the start. He penned:

Mrs. Gronewald and Mrs. McCordic, our paid museum
attendants, worked at least one day a week for a year,
without pay, in order to get the museum items cataloged.
A number of other volunteer[s]...worked every Thursday...
in order to have the museum presentable for the opening
date...we all appreciate and thank them heartily for their
labor of love.

Today, our volunteers, staff, and board continue to
demonstrate that same "labor of love" for our museum. This
effort is evident as we see the continued expansion of our
exhibits across Clark County under the guidance and leadership
of our Public Historian, Katie Bush. In this year, we added an
additional six panels in Historic Downtown Camas. These
panels tell the stories of some of Camas' most historic buildings
and historical figures. We also partnered with Riverview Bank
to create traveling exhibit panels for their 100th Anniversary.
These panels move from branch to branch, helping Clark County
residents and beyond understand this vital bank's incredible
story. Furthermore, we added our first new exhibit inside the
museum since 2020. The "Homegrown Historians" exhibition
explores our community's story through the images and words
of historians, photographers, storytellers, and writers. The
center of this exhibit showcases work from students from Our
Lady of Lourdes School in Vancouver.

Brougher further discussed the initial donations that started
our collection. Today, the museum receives treasured pieces of
our history under our Collections Manager, Liza Schade. This
year's first addition to our collection was a commemorative
souvenir pen set given to Clark County's historian and former
Vancouver City Council Member Pat Jollota. Pat received this
gift in conjunction with commemorating the 100th birthday
of Russian Air Force test pilot, Valery Chkalov. This gift came
to Pat in her capacity as a Vancouver City Council Member.

This year, other pieces of history brought into our care include a dress uniform from Major General Curtis Loop, a collection from former Washington State Representative and Speaker of the House for the State of Washington Robert Schaefer, and the Marquee sign for the Monterey Hotel. These are just a handful of the new objects taken under our care in 2023.

Lastly, Dr. Brougher notes the first programs. He outlined that:

Our first program of the year was in March, at which time, Mr. and Mrs. Marchall Dana presented in conversational style "Tid-Bits of Northwest History." In April our speaker was s…[the] archivist for Washington State University.

Over this last year, through the design and delivery of our Outreach and Public Programs Manager, April Buzby, we saw the expansion of our community-centered programming initiative. The Speaker Series today provides insightful looks into the many stories that make up the mosaic of our community. Our newest program, #CCHMuseum After Hours, supports our community partners by providing a platform for community building, public engagement, and outreach based on their needs. Also, History on Tap dove into the contributions of our BIPOC community.

As we embark on our 60th year of operation, I can't thank our community enough for its continued support over these decades. Our daily endeavor to save our stories would not be possible without a passionate and engaged community. We are proud of what the past six decades have brought and ready to celebrate what the next six decades will bring.

Bradley Richardson
Executive Director

ARTICLES

The checkered past of Clark County's own railroad

Native Americans' mystery route, a future Civil War general, bankruptcy, double suicide, complex string of ownerships, the St. Paul string-puller, and historic wildfire—all were part of the Chelatchie Prairie Railroad's fascinating story.

Gregg Herrington

In the beginning

You might say the saga of the 33-mile railroad running southwest to northeast across Clark County began hundreds of years ago. Native Americans regularly crossed the Cascade Mountains between Southwest Washington and the Yakima Valley on a route that came to be known as the Klickitat Trail.

Today, the ancient Klickitat Trail is vaguely identifiable in places and lost in others. But its importance to the first inhabitants of the region helped inspire the creation in 1887 of the Vancouver, Klickitat & Yakima Railroad (VK&Y). Today, it's a county-owned line with a for-profit freight operation on the south end and an all-volunteer excursion line in the north.

Or, we might say the story of the VK&Y began in 1853 when U. S. Army Capt. George McClellan, who would briefly serve as commanding general of the Union Army in the Civil War, was assigned to search for a future rail route through the Cascade Range. So, on July 18, 1853, he led a party of 66 men plus horses and pack animals from Columbia Barracks (aka "Fort Vancouver") to look for a potential rail route. McClellan headed northeast to "Yalicolt," the Klickitat Indians' name for today's Yacolt. From there, McClellan went on to Chelatchie Prairie, then east up the free-flowing North Fork of the Lewis River into the Cascade Range. The ancient Native Americans' Klickitat Trail is widely thought to have gone over the crest of the Cascades north of the McClellan route, between the White Salmon River and the Klickitat River drainages.

By most accounts, McClellan was not a happy camper. His descriptions of his route ranged mostly from difficult to miserable and "too expensive for railroad construction."

It would be another decade before Congress and President Lincoln chartered the Northern Pacific Railroad on July 2,

Chelatchie Prairie RR excursion train pulls out of Yacolt on Aug. 19, 2023. Brakeman watches track ahead from caboose while in radio contact with engineer. On return trip caboose will be at rear. (Photo by author)

1864 (reincorporated August 31, 1896, as the Northern Pacific Railway) to build a line from the Great Lakes to Puget Sound. In 1878 and 1880, NP surveyors studied possible routes in eastern Lewis County up the Cowlitz River drainage near today's Packwood, crossing the crest somewhere in the White Pass (U. S. Highway 12) area. But the railroad dismissed the notion of a crossing that far south and turned its attention northward. In 1881 Northern Pacific Railroad civil engineer Virgil Bogue discovered Stampede Pass—two miles south of today's Interstate 90 Snoqualmie Pass—over the Cascades to Tacoma. That route is still used by the BNSF, successor to the NP and others.

Nevertheless, back in Vancouver in the mid-1880s, the dream of a cross-Cascades rail route from Clarke County, as it was then spelled, to the Yakima Valley lived on. We could find no definitive written or mapped route the Vancouver investors might have envisioned for their proposed railroad to Yakima. But based on McClellan's expedition plus documents, books, diaries and interviews with back-country hikers, railroad historians and U.S. Forest Service retirees, the presumed rail route would have followed this route—more or less:

Chelatchie Prairie north to the North Fork of the free-flowing Lewis River...east from the south side of today's Yale Reservoir up to McClellan Meadows in the Gifford Pinchot National Forest...through the Indian Heaven Wilderness Area...down near the community of Trout Lake and across the White Salmon River...south of Mount Adams into the Klickitat River drainage...past today's community of Glenwood then over the Klickitat River...northeast into Yakima County to or near Fort Simcoe and White Swan and 17 miles to North Yakima (today's Yakima). There, as the Vancouver dreamers saw things, it would connect to the Northern Pacific Railroad's line north to Ellensburg and Tacoma or east to Pasco, Spokane and the Midwest.

Included in the unrealized dream of the VK&Y founders was a branch line from western Klickitat County to Goldendale. There was even talk of connecting the line from Vancouver to the Manitoba line of the Canadian National Railway at Yakima, creating a transcontinental connection. But it didn't happen. Not even close.

False starts

February 12, 1883—Several prominent Vancouver men invested $250,000 total to incorporate the Northwestern Railroad and Improvement Co. with the intention of building a rail line that would "extend from Vancouver through Clark County in a northeasterly direction." Among the organizers were Lowell M. Hidden and future Vancouver Mayor Charles Brown. The dream was abandoned before a single rail was laid.

February 23, 1885—The **Vancouver & Yakima Railroad** ("Klickitat" was not in the name) was incorporated and capitalized for $750,000 by well-connected local men, including many of those involved in the earlier effort, plus Eugene Semple of Vancouver, a former governor of Washington Territory. They signed the incorporation papers in the Vancouver office of Notary Public William Byron Daniels, whose family was the namesake of Daniels Street in West Vancouver. Again, work on the line was never begun.

But the dream still did not die. On July 8, 1886, L.M. Hidden led a half dozen Vancouver men on the start of a pack trip northeast via Yacolt into the Cascade Mountains and kept a detailed diary of the month-long trip. A Hidden family history written in 1954 by L.M. Hidden's grandson, the late Robert A. Hidden, says, "The purpose of the trip was to find a possible route for a R.R. to Yakima and see what the timber was."

However, the diary itself concentrates on timber, berries, fishing, hunting and the camping experience, not potential railroad routes.

Then, finally...

January 29, 1887— The Vancouver, Klickitat & Yakima Railroad (VK&Y) was launched when these men appeared in William Daniels' office to sign papers of incorporation: Samuel W. Brown, Charles Brown, William H. Brewster, Lynn B. Clough, Lowell M. Hidden, banker Edmund L. Canby, brewery owner Anton Young, Patrick O'Keane, William Smiley, Harvey H. Gridley, Loring C. Palmer and David Schuele. Among other principals in the new railroad were Louis Sohns and Peter C. McFarlane. (Remember that name: McFarlane.)

If these incorporators included any experienced railroad owners, executives, contractors, builders, civil engineers, geologists, or back-country surveyors, it was not apparent. Capitalized for $1 million, the company's stated purpose was "to construct and equip a railroad and telegraph line from the city of Vancouver in the county of Clarke...in a generally northeasterly direction through the Klickitat or other available pass in the Cascade range of mountains to the coal mines situated in said mountains...to a junction with the Cascade Branch of the Northern Pacific Railroad at or near the city of North Yakima (today's Yakima)...and to carry freight and passengers thereon." The document also stated a goal of building a branch line from western Klickitat County southeast to Goldendale.

November 26, 1887—*Railway World* cheered the creation of the VK&Y, declaring, "The grades are feasible and easy...as soon as the necessary capital can be enlisted construction will commence."

December 22, 1887—The *Register* gushed, "The dawn is breaking. Vancouver has a great future....The VK&Y "will run to the coal fields near Mt. Adams—tapping the finest body of yellow fir, cedar and larch on the Pacific coast, and opening up to settlement thousands of acres....The road will be continued to some point in Eastern Washington, bringing to Vancouver for

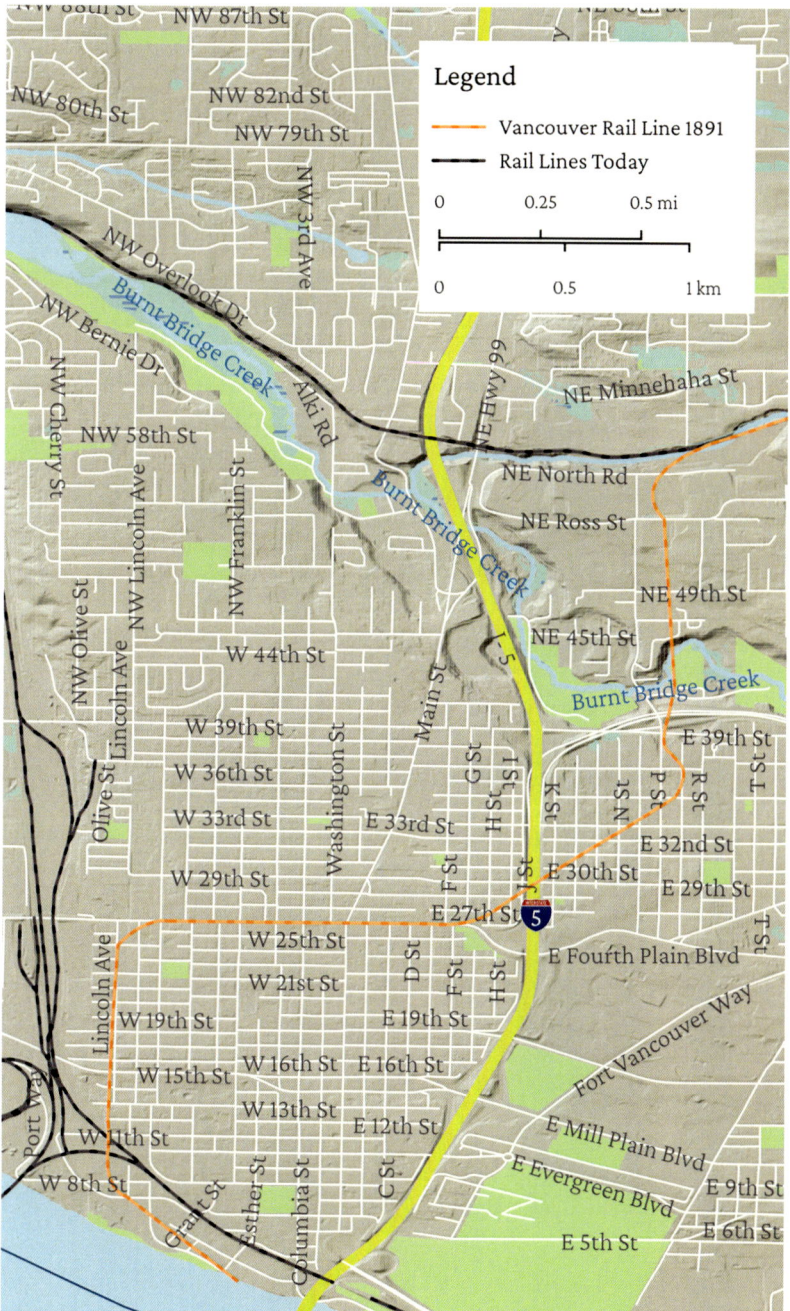

The railroad's 33-mile route, from its junction with the BNSF mainline near NE 78th Street and Lake Shore Avenue on the west to Chelatchie in northeast Clark County. (Map by April Buzby)

shipment the products of Klickitat, Yakima and other sections of the inland empire."

Route through Vancouver

From the south, the VK&Y route began on the Columbia River waterfront near a sawmill and the ferry landing at the foot of today's Washington Street, then ran:
Northwest to today's Lincoln Avenue (then named Railroad Avenue)
North to W. 26th Street (today's Fourth Plain Boulevard)
East on 26th to G Street in the Arnada neighborhood
Northeast through today's Rose Village (previously the Rosemere Neighborhood), passing what would one day be Interstate 5 at 29th Street and continuing northeasterly approximately to E. 39th and P streets.
North down and over Burnt Bridge Creek and northeast to N.E. 19th Avenue, then northeast to cross St. Johns Boulevard at N.E. 68th Street.
(Author's note: This route was pieced together with the considerable help of Bob Weaver of the Pacific Northwest Chapter of the National Railway Historical Society, Doug Auburg, Pat Jollota and Jerry Olson.)

Ownership mystery

On Page 346, Volume I, of *No More Bells, Nor Whistles*—a History of Washington Railroads by Paul D. Curtiss, it says the railroad was incorporated on January 29, 1887, "in the Washington Territory, as a wholly owned subsidiary of the Michigan Lumber Co."
The *Michigan* **Lumber Company?** Who and what is that? What about those businessmen who signed the papers of incorporation? Curtiss was tracked down by phone. He said he didn't remember his source for the ownership assertion and that he couldn't swear to the accuracy of the thousands of names, dates, numbers etc., in his three massive volumes of Washington railroad and streetcar history.

There was a Michigan Lumber Co. in Vancouver that did have a close relationship with the VK&Y. Battle Ground historian Don Higgins found a link in *The Illustrated History of the State of Washington* in 1993 by H. K. Hines. It states on Page 373 that the VK&Y Railroad "is owned and controlled by the stockholders of the Michigan Lumber Co." rather than by the lumber company itself.

Peter C. McFarlane, a Michigan native, was the lumber company's well-connected president. His son, Charles McFarlane, was secretary and treasurer. McFarlane was also an investor in residential land development along the VK&Y route. By 1891 he was president of the VK&Y itself and a member of the Vancouver City Council.

As reported by *The Vancouver Independent*, the Michigan Lumber Co. began operations here in August 1889 "to take care of logs brought in by the VK&Y railway." It had at least two sawmills in the area, including one in Sara a few miles south of Ridgefield, and the largest mill in Vancouver on the Columbia River waterfront just downstream from the site of today's Interstate 5 Bridge.

Things were going well...

January 28, 1888—The contract for clearing the first five miles of the VK&Y route went to Malone & Co. of Butte, Mont. Work began three days later.

May 4, 1888—*The Washington Standard* of Olympia reported, "About 250 Chinamen have been put to work on the Vancouver, Klickitat & Yakima railroad. The rolling stock and iron for the first 20 miles has been ordered."

May 13, 1888—*The Salem Statesman Journal* reported from Vancouver that "Mahone (sic) & Co. finished their contract today of grading and laying the Vancouver, Klickitat & Yakima Railroad for the first five miles."

By the end of 1888, the first locomotive for the VK&Y arrived from Pittsburgh. A week later, 17 cars of rolling stock arrived.

According to a history of the railroad by Walt Ainsworth, "The VK&Y hauled logs from camps along the line to mills in Vancouver, or to the Columbia River to be rafted and towed to other mills. Operated as a logging railroad, the line proved to be a profitable investment for the first few years." (Northern Pacific Railway Historical Association's *The Mainstreeter* magazine, Spring 1992)

November 11, 1889—Washington became a state.

Until they weren't...

September 7, 1888—The young company was in financial trouble and work on the line had come to a halt. VK&Y stockholders voted "to diminish the company's capital stock" to $60,000. The notarized record of that meeting says "all of the stockholders" were represented. A dozen eager Vancouver capitalists had been in on the incorporation in January 1887. But

Clark County's first locomotive, delivered to the short-lived Vancouver, Klickitat & Yakima Railroad in 1888 by Porter Brothers Locomotive Works in Pittsburgh. (Source: Clark County Historical Museum cmpn00056)

19 months later, "All" of the stockholders apparently numbered only five: Louis Sohns, L. M. Hidden, William H. Brewster, D. F. Schuele and Charles Brown.

November 11, 1889—Washington became a state.

Christmas Day, 1891—*The Portland Telegram* reported, "Negotiations for the Vancouver, Klickitat & Yakima railroad are progressing as fast as possible, which will be welcome news to many Portland people who are interested in this new railroad."

But there also were ominous economic developments nationally, including the failure of the huge Reading Railroad and the infamous bank panic of 1893.

August 8, 1893 —"The lumber business has gone flat," *The Vancouver Independent* declared. "The mills of this city are not running more than one-third of the time."

Three days later, the local Superior Court was petitioned to appoint a receiver to wind up the affairs of the Michigan Lumber Co. in Vancouver. The petition said two mortgages totaling $45,000 were executed by the company through P. C. McFarlane, its president, in favor of himself, without the consent of the other trustees.

December 31, 1893—"The times are hard—harder than ever." The Vancouver Register editorialized on New Year's Eve. "Under the iniquitous gold standard, property values and wages have been cut fully in half. Hundreds of people in this county—are out of employment. Taxes are high, and—no money."

Whidbey Island, Wash., historian and author Robert W. Merry, in his biography of President William McKinley, writes that the national recession and the 1893 bank panic amounted to "a great economic cataclysm" that led to the failure of 600 banks and 74 railroads.

April 20, 1894—*The Railroad Gazette* reported, "Sale of the VK&Y is being negotiated by local directors to an Eastern firm which proposes to extend the line and develop timber lands along the line." But no "Eastern firm" materialized—at least not publicly. The VK&Y lingered. It had built the line only 13 miles from Vancouver to Brush Prairie.

February 2, 1897—*The Railroad Gazette* reported that former Vancouver Mayor R. W. Stapleton had been appointed receiver upon application of the principal bondholders and the original intention of the VK&Y stretching over the Cascades to Yakima had not been realized "because of a lack of capital."

Enter: The PV&Y

The nail in the coffin of the VK&Y was driven on November 30, 1897. But the Yakima dream was not yet dead—at least not publicly. *The Vancouver Weekly Columbian* reported the company "was sold at receiver's sale, by order of the Superior Court. Prospective buyers were reported to be an unnamed "party of capitalists" who hope to "extend it to Yakima."

"The old Vancouver, Klickitat & Yakima railroad is no more," *The Vancouver Independent declared* on December 2, 1897. It was now the Portland, Vancouver & Yakima Railway Co. (PV&Y). For the prominent Vancouver businessmen and political figures who had been present at its creation ten years earlier, the VK&Y had been a bad investment.

The new, smaller PV&Y Board of Trustees comprised Louis Gerlinger Sr., his son George T. Gerlinger, both of Vancouver, and James H. Hubbard of Portland. (The Gerlingers would later establish the Gerlinger Motor Car Co. in Portland, progenitor of Kenworth Trucks, and the Willamette Valley Lumber Co., which became Willamette Industries.)

As far as the public knew, reaching Yakima with the PV&Y was still the goal. On December 3, 1897, *The Columbian* said the new unnamed owners intended "at once to extend the road (from Salmon Creek) to Chelatchie Prairie" and thus "open up the finest timber belt on the Pacific Coast, and, in addition, an extensive bituminous coal field"...and eventually "continue the main line of the road to North Yakima and a branch to Goldendale...The taking hold of so important an enterprise shows the faith that men of means have in the future of the great Northwest." On the other hand, *The Railroad Gazette* did not mention Yakima in its December 17, 1897, story about the same event.

We tracked down John Boule, archivist at the Yakima Valley Historical Museum. We asked if there had been any anticipation and enthusiasm from the public or business community there about the prospect of a Vancouver-to-Yakima railroad. Boule did some research and reported back: "I cannot see any great swelling of support" for the VK&Y or its successor, the PV&Y. "I see no major Yakima participation."

In the meantime, the PV&Y increased its initial issue of 500 shares of capital stock valued at $50,000 to 2,000 shares valued at $200,000. Where did that money come from? Who was really in charge?

Enter: 'The Empire Builder'

That would be James J. Hill, "The Empire Builder" of St. Paul, Minn. He had founded the Great Northern Railway—the

Vancouver Mayor John P. Kiggins (center back) next to James J. Hill (right) at Vancouver railroad depot, Oct. 4, 1911. Depot, at west end of 11th Street, is still in operation. (Source: Clark County Historical Museum cchm07328)

SP&S AND THE DEATH OF A DREAM

It's unclear just when James J. Hill in St. Paul, Minn., or I.N. Gray, his top man on the ground in Vancouver, ended the hope of a railroad from Vancouver going over the Cascade Mountains to Yakima. There's scant—if any—evidence Hill ever really bought into the notion.

But these factors likely convinced Hill to cut the cord on the dream:

Geography

This alone might have been sufficient to end consideration of an over-the-mountains railroad. We couldn't find proof that a detailed map ever existed showing a credible planned route, including the point a train would cross a presumed "Klickitat Pass" into Eastern Washington.

But a rail route along the Washington side of the Columbia River—the future "North Bank Road" of the Spokane, Portland and Seattle Railway—was lower and flatter, thus easier and cheaper to build, maintain and use, with fewer locomotives needed. The route along the river ranges from an elevation of about 40 feet in Vancouver to 190 feet at Maryhill, 110 miles east. A mountain-pass would likely have been 3,000-4,000 feet above sea level.

Today, no railroad crosses the Cascades anywhere between Stampede Pass (Ellensburg to Seattle) and the original SP&S line along the Washington side of the Columbia River.

Conservation vs Extraction

The first major public environmental debate in the Pacific Northwest was brewing. It might have caught the attention of Hill and added to doubts about an over-the-Cascades route.

Boundaries and restrictions on the Mount Rainier Forest Reserve—predecessor to the Gifford Pinchot National Forest—were being wrangled and lobbied in Congress, public forums and within the executive branch of government. It pitted conservationists vs. the timber and mining industries in an early preview of future battles, including the raging spotted owl controversy of the late 1980s into the 1990s.

Lawrence Rakestraw grew up in Carson, Wash., near the Gifford Pinchot National Forest. He attended Washougal High School and Clark College. In 1955 he wrote his doctoral thesis at the University of Washington on the history of Pacific Northwest forest conservation. This passage in his paper might be all we need to know about why no railroad—regardless of its owners—was built from Clark County over the Cascades to Yakima:

In 1901 the Northern Pacific began building its North Bank (of the Columbia River) Road, and the value of the PV&Y charter disappeared. The next year the Yacolt fire swept over much of the area and rendered the Lewis River area less valuable for timber... Perhaps the deciding factor was the large amount of alienated land owned by the State, the Northern Pacific, and the Weyerhaeuser (Timber Co.) interests in the area.

"Alienated land"—There's an elegant term for what would have been a controversial railroad route through the Cascades.

A page 1 story in The Morning Oregonian of July 27, 1901, bluntly concluded the Northern Pacific's North Bank route to Vancouver and eventually over a railroad bridge to Portland "would leave the Portland, Vancouver & Yakima Railroad without transcontinental significance."

The Yacolt Burn

Rakestraw also suggested in his 1955 thesis that the 1902 fire could have been another factor weighing against the over-the-Cascades dream, giving pause to a railroad owner who would have wanted to sell standing timber on his route.

On March 11, 1908, the North Bank Road completion was celebrated with a golden spike ceremony at Sheridan's Point, between today's Bridge of the Gods and Bonneville Dam. The first passenger train over the new route, with ten coaches and 500 guests, had left Vancouver that morning for the event.

The Spokane Spokesman-Review reported, "The exercises were short but impressive, and when the last stroke of the gilded hammer died away, cheer after cheer was flung into the air and the Inland Empire at last had direct connection with the great Columbia harbor."

On March 19, 1908, daily passenger service from Vancouver to Pasco began, with connections to Spokane and then east to the Great Lakes region. A week later, the double-track SP&S bridge in Vancouver opened. Trains from east and north crossed the Columbia River to Portland's iconic Union Station with its 150-foot Romanesque Revival clocktower. A neon sign on the tower says, "Go By Train."

Stock Certificate for Portland, Vancouver & Yakima RR, issued Dec. 28, 1897, to Louis Gerlinger. One month earlier, the PV&Y replaced the bankrupt Vancouver, Klickitat & Yakima Railroad and resumed building the line to Yacolt. (Source: Don Higgins)

company with "Rocky," the mountain goat, as its corporate symbol. The rival Northern Pacific Railway had been financially ailing, and Hill was acquiring stock and gaining power through its subsidiaries and affiliates.

Don Higgins of Battle Ground is a history sleuth rich in curiosity, patience and arcane sources. He discovered an April 13, 1901, edition of *The Railroad and Engineering Review* that reported Isaac N. Gray, who was linked to Hill back in Minnesota, had been elected president and treasurer of the PV&Y for the coming year.

Assessing the changes at the top of the PV&Y, Higgins concluded, "Louis Gerlinger, who had been president, was essentially demoted to vice president. Gerlinger's son George, who had been secretary, was now on the outside looking in. James J. Hill, who was not named in the PV&Y incorporation papers, had his fingerprints all over this change." Indeed, he did. Fingerprints and boot tracks.

Hill was physically imposing, enterprising, impatient and powerful. His business tentacles were spread all over the upper Midwest and across the northern tier to Seattle.

Hill had acquired an interest in the financially troubled Northern Pacific Railway, which, as it turned out, was the power behind the throne at the new PV&Y Railroad. From off stage, Hill was influencing—or making decisions for—the PV&Y.

Gray, Kettenring head west

One might imagine Hill, the tough businessman who knew something about building railroads, back in his St. Paul office, pacing and harrumphing about under-financed amateurs running the little railroad out in Clark County, Washington.

In 1900, Hill sent newlywed I. N. (Isaac Newton) Gray with his bride, Margaret McLean Gray, to take over as president of the new line. In 1901, F.M. Kettenring was sent from Minnesota to supervise the construction of the line north to Yacolt. Kettenring's granddaughter, Karen Kettenring Caplinger of Battle Ground, continues the story:

> Grandma Katherine McLean (Kate when she was young) was introduced to F. M. Kettenring (Fred) by his best friend I. N. Gray in Minnesota. Fred and Kate dated in Duluth when he had days off from various railroad projects. Both men would have Sunday dinners with the sisters at the McLean home. The Grays were married in Minnesota and came to Vancouver together. Fred came alone a year later to be construction director for the PV&Y. He subsequently asked Kate to follow, and they were married in Vancouver on Thanksgiving, 1901.

Gray would be the well-connected face of the PV&Y, the one in the suit making political connections and doing Hill's bidding. Kettenring, a professional civil engineer and surveyor, would be the on-sight construction supervisor.

Higgins, the Battle Ground historian, says, "The railroad barons of that day went to great lengths to keep their business private and away from their competitors, even to the extent of deliberately misnaming a railroad to avoid competition for rights-of-way. It is undeniable that Northern Pacific, which Hill controlled, owned all the shares of the PV&Y before July of 1903."

April 19, 1901, double suicide—Vancouver bankers Charles Brown and Edmund Canby, who had been among the founders of the Vancouver, Klickitat & Yakima Railroad and whose bank was associated with the VK&Y, committed suicide when a bank examiner discovered wrongdoing and the bank failed.

July 13, 1901—with Gray now in charge, the Portland, Vancouver & Yakima Railroad was folded into the Washington Railway and Navigation Co. The WR&N was a family of railroads linked to the Northern Pacific Railway, which was very much linked to James J. Hill in St. Paul, Minn.

BANKERS WITH VK&Y LINKS TAKE OWN LIVES

On April 19, 1901, a tragic piece of Vancouver's history had a connection to the complex story of the Chelatchie Prairie Railroad. It made Page 1 in the April 22, 1901, edition of The New York Times under this headline:

BANKERS COMMIT SUICIDE
Two Officers of Suspended Vancouver Bank Shoot Themselves.
Confessed that They Were Responsible for $81,000 Shortage—Army Officer the Principal Stockholder.

Charles Brown, 54, was secretary-treasurer of the short-lived railroad when it was incorporated as the Vancouver, Klickitat & Yakima R.R. in 1887. He later became president of the First National Bank of Vancouver.

Edmund Canby, 52, another VK&Y incorporator, was the bank's cashier. As such, he was responsible for bank money, both received and expended. The bank itself was listed on incorporation papers as treasurer of the VK&Y.

Brown and his wife lived in one of Vancouver's most elegant homes at 400 W. 11th St. The refurbished structure today is home to the Vancouver office of the Stahancy, Kent & Hook law firm. The firm's website (charlesbrownhouse.com) has the story of the bank scandal and the suicides:

During the boom years of 1889 and 1890, the bank loaned too much money on insufficient funds. Brown and Canby made false entries in the books over the

July 27, 1901—There was probably a specific time and place the dream of the PV&Y going over the Cascades to Yakima was put to death. But the primary reason was no mystery. A page 1 story in *The Morning Oregonian* concluded the Northern Pacific's North Bank of the Columbia River route from Pasco to Vancouver —and eventually over a railroad bridge to Portland—"would leave the Portland, Vancouver & Yakima Railroad without transcontinental significance." The North Bank Route became the Spokane, Portland& Seattle Railway Co.

'You scratch my back and . . .'

Don Higgins asks: "Why was the Big Guy [Hill] stepping in to change management [of the PV&Y] and extend the railway to Yacolt on, what was to him, a small and distant operation?"

First, know this: When the Northern Pacific was chartered in 1864, the government committed to pay for construction by giving the NP 46 million acres of federal land in states it crossed.

subsequent years to cover up the bad transactions.

One of the bad loans had been $20,000 to the Michigan Lumber Co. Other heavy losers included the Portland, Vancouver, & Yakima Railway ($2,000), successor to the Vancouver, Klickitat & Yakima Railway. The Army officer referenced in the headline was Col. Stephen P. Jocelyn, of San Francisco but stationed in Vancouver when the bank was organized in 1883 "and ever since that time he has been the heaviest stockholder."

Bank Inspector J. W. Maxwell determined the bank to be insolvent and ordered it closed.

According to The Vancouver Independent, the bank had about 1,000 depositors with only $230,000 in deposits, and there had been no dividend paid since 1895.

According to the newspaper, both men kept the state of the bank a secret for more than a decade. It was not until April of 1901 when Bank Examiner Maxwell discovered their secret and confronted both men. "After confessing to the examiner, Brown and Canby, racked with guilt, walked to a nearby field on the edge of town and committed suicide with the same pistol."

This note was found on Canby:

My Dear Wife: I feel that what I am about to do is for the best. Forgive me if you can, and try to live for our dear children. God bless you all! Forgive me.

April 19, 1901, E.L. Canby

The NP's eventual route over the Cascades to Tacoma was timber-rich.

Higgins suggests an answer to his question about why Hill was so interested in the little railroad in Clarke County:

> On January 3, 1900, Frederick Weyerhaeuser and several partners bought 900,000 acres [1,406 square miles] of prime Washington state timberland from the Northern Pacific for $5.4 million. Two weeks later, The Weyerhaeuser Timber Co. was incorporated in Washington State. Hill had just exercised his new control of the Northern Pacific to sell his friend [and St. Paul neighbor] Frederick Weyerhaeuser great tracts of Washington timberland in one of the largest private land transfers in U.S. history...Making Weyerhaeuser successful helped make Hill successful.

For example, listed among the real estate transactions in the *Vancouver Weekly Columbian* on December 17, 1903, was this evidence of a Hill-Weyerhaeuser symbiotic relationship: "Northern Pacific Ry. Co. to Weyerhaeuser Timber Co., 178.43 acres in Sec.1, T. 4 N., R 4 E.; $931.37."

A tunnel, a bridge, a fire

In 1901, with Gray and Kettenring on the job, work on the line had continued apace. On September 3, 1901, *The Vancouver Independent* reported from Yacolt, "Grading on the PV&Y is progressing very fast. Two miles at this end will be completed tomorrow.

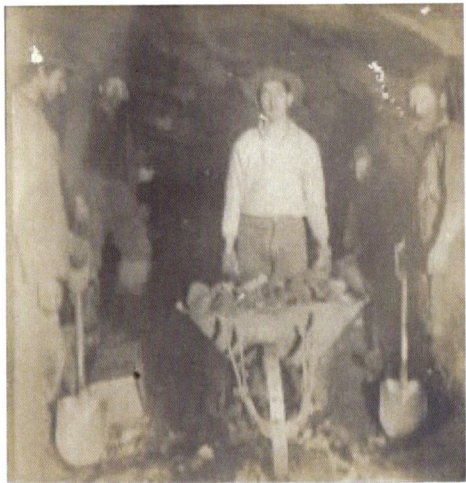

Digging the Portland, Vancouver, & Yakima Railroad tunnel. (Source: Karen Kettenring Caplinger)

In 1961, F. M. Kettenring's widow, Katherine, wrote that her husband's "major challenges were putting a (342-foot) tunnel through the stone formation flanking the East Fork of the Lewis River (near Moulton Falls) and building a bridge" over the East Fork of the Lewis River, downstream from Lucia Falls.

Katherine Kettenring also wrote that as her husband and Gray had been absorbed in finishing the railroad to Yacolt, "the terrible Yacolt fire of 1902 blinded all who were in its vicinity with the pall of smoke and cinders." Completing the tunnel would have to wait.

Wikipedia describes the Yacolt Burn as "the collective name for dozens of fires in Washington state and Oregon occurring between September 8 and September 12, 1902..." *The Vancouver Independent* calls it "The greatest tragedy ever witnessed in Clarke County....The distress and desolation is awful to behold."

Fires were not a one-time threat. Katherine Kettenring later wrote about the day a subsequent fire threatened the family and

Portland, Vancouver & Yakima Railroad tunnel after 1902 Yacolt Burn. (Source: Karen Kettenring Caplinger)

its sawmill three-quarters of a mile upstream of Lucia Falls on the East Fork:

> We soon could see the flames in the forest behind our homes and the roar of the fire became terrifying, so we fled with our children to the mill pond....By 2:00 p.m., it was dark and necessary to use lanterns to care for the children on the cots. The crackling blazes sent firebrands (pieces of burning wood) and cinders across the pond, and we were busy picking burning brands off the cots and sprinkling the covers to keep our little ones from burning. Only the pond lay between us and destruction.

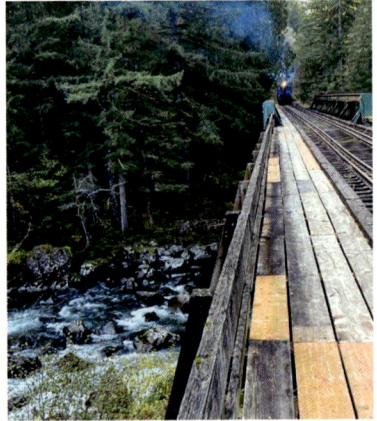

Excursion train, powered by steam locomotive, approaches East Fork Lewis River bridge on return trip to Yacolt. (Source: Battle Ground, Yacolt, Chelatchie Prairie Railroad)

The fire claimed 65 lives, 38 of them in the Lewis River drainage. It destroyed 238,900 acres, most in Clark, Cowlitz and Skamania counties, stopping just short of Yacolt. Wildfires would also plague the area in subsequent years, the largest being the 1929 Yacolt Burn, aka the Dole Fire, which scorched 227,500 acres.

Yacolt, the end of the line

After the fire, the push to complete the track to Yacolt resumed. But the specific date a locomotive entered the town for the first time could not be ascertained, not even the year. This important date in Yacolt's history could only be narrowed to sometime between late November 1902 and the middle of January 1903.

January 8, 1903—*The Vancouver Independent* reported, "The little town of Yacolt at the end of the PV&Y road is experiencing quite a boom. Two logging camps have recently started nearby, and more to follow. Petitions for licenses for two saloons have been filed...Other metropolitan features are soon to be added." But when was "recently?" Late 1902 or early 1903?

Louise McKay Allworth Tucker, author of *Battle Ground: In and Around*, dug up a book she had read years ago and almost forgotten: *From Jamestown to Coffin Rock—a History of Weyerhaeuser Operations in Southwest Washingto*n, by Alden H. Jones, 1974. Here's a crucial passage from Jones' book:

> Jim Salovich, who was to become a logging camp legend, was the interpreter for the Austrians and the Slovakians who worked on the track-laying gang, which pushed the end of steel into Yacolt Prairie in January, 1903.

> The "Y" for "Yakima" in PV&Y remained emblazoned in large white letters on its black steam locomotives. But as far as proud locals were concerned, the Y stood for "Yacolt."

Flume over East Fork of the Lewis River carried lumber to the railroad near present-day Heisson Store. (Source: Ceci Ryan Smith)

Logging camps and sawmills

After the fire and with the PV&Y completed to Yacolt, sawmills and logging camps thrived in the heavily forested north county. Some operations included railroad spur lines into the foothills of the Cascade Range. The Weyerhaeuser Timber Co. launched a considerable salvage operation through subsidiaries Clarke County Timber Company and Twin Falls Logging Company.

Flumes were built to carry logs and lumber to the railroad. A magnificent flume, thought to have been designed by F. M. Kettenring, carried logs from the Ryan-Allen logging camp on the north side of the Lewis River's East Fork, across the river to the railroad stop near the present Heisson Store for the trip by rail to a Vancouver mill. (Four different spellings of Heisson have been used by various entities. The railroad spelling was Heison, but Heisson has emerged as the most enduring.)

The May 1912 edition of *The Timberman* magazine, published in Portland, included brief items about three mills dependent on the PV&Y: The F.M. Kettenring and Huston-brothers Lucia Mill three-quarters of a mile upstream from Lucia Falls; Kettenring's Dole Valley Mill; the Ryan-Allen logging operation, north from Heisson across the East Fork of the Lewis River, operated by N. E. Allen, M. L. Ryan and C. W. Ryan. Ceci Ryan Smith of Vancouver, long active in Vancouver's historic preservation efforts who helped with research for this story, is a granddaughter of C. W. "Cicero" Ryan.

The trains routinely hauled logs or lumber to mills or the docks in Vancouver. But Dave Spau of St. Helens, Ore., now retired after 40 years as a railroad man, says there was another offloading possibility: "log dumps" in local waterways to await transfer by towboats to points as far away as Seattle and San Francisco.

Moving right along

At the same time, things were happening fast on the NP's main line north from Vancouver:

Remains of pilings in Burnt Bridge Creek that once carried tracks east to Yacolt from mainline along Lake Shore Avenue. Rails in foreground on north bank of the creek now provide only link to BNSF main line nearby. (Photo by author)

February 6, 1903—The bridge over the Lewis River in Woodland was completed, and its first train rolled into Vancouver from Kalama.

March 1, 1903—Northern Pacific began regular passenger service between Vancouver and Kalama and, from there, north to Tacoma.

April 1, 1903—Pacific Construction Co. was awarded the contract to extend the Yacolt line 3.37 miles from Hidden Station (later renamed Rye Station) near St. Johns Boulevard and N.E. 68th Street). When completed, the extension would be a direct route west from Rye to the Northern Pacific's main north-south line at Vancouver Junction, a few feet west of Lake Shore Avenue and just south of N.W. 78th Street. The junction is still in use. When Vancouver Junction was completed, PV&Y trains would no longer run through several Vancouver residential neighborhoods now named Rose Village, Shumway, Arnada, Upper Main and Hough.

August 31, 1903—Regular service began over the new leg from near Hidden Station along the north side of Burnt Bridge Creek to the main north-south line at Vancouver Junction.

Here, from *Battle Ground: In and Around*, were the regular stops along the PV&Y line, west to east, after the new leg opened:

Vancouver Junction—Just north of the mouth of Burnt Bridge Creek adjacent to Lake Shore Avenue.

Hidden—(Later named Rye) N.E. 68th Street and St. John's Blvd.

Barberton —NE 72nd Ave. and 99th Street

Homan—NE 87th Ave. and 110th Street.

Laurin— East of Glenwood Hts. Primary School at N.E. 134th St and Laurin Road (Initially called "Gravel Pit.") Brush Prairie, Caples Road, south of Brush Prairie General Store.

Battle Ground—Main Street at the east end of downtown, where Kettenring would establish a retail lumber yard in 1924.

Crawford—N.E. 249th Street at the entrance to Battle Ground Lake State Park.

Heisson—Near Heisson Store at 279th St. and 176th Ave. The railroad spelling is Heison.

Wall—Along East Fork Lewis River near Lucia Falls.

Lucia—At the Lucia mill, about three-quarters of a mile upstream from Heisson Bridge.

Moulton—Dole Mill, near Big Tree Creek's confluence with East Fork Lewis River.

Yacolt—East side of town on Railroad Avenue.

October 19, 1903—With James J. Hill in St. Paul pulling the strings on the PV&Y, it was folded into the Washington Railway and Navigation Co. (WR&N), a family of railroads linked to the Northern Pacific Railway, which was controlled by Hill, who had founded the Great Northern Railway and came to be known as The Empire Builder.

November 14, 1903—A passenger coach was added to the one train daily between Vancouver and Yacolt. A one-way ticket was $1.07. Passengers previously rode in the caboose or freight cars.

Extraction has its limits

Logging and lumber were booming for sure. But trees are an exhaustible resource. By the end of the decade, the salvageable timber left over from the 1902 Yacolt Burn was nearly gone. In 1917 the Twin Falls Logging Co. sold its assets and departed. In 1918 the Ryan-Allen operation at Heisson shut down and moved to Hoquiam. The logging of green timber continued in the area but was waning by the mid-1920s.

December 23, 1925—The Washington Legislature corrected a longstanding spelling error and officially changed Clarke County to Clark County.

December 4, 1929 —Weyerhaeuser Timber Co. General Manager George S. Long informed stockholders that its subsidiary in the Yacolt area, the Clark County Timber Co., was closing. In his grim, glass-is-almost-empty statement, Long said, "At Yacolt we have two or three worn out buildings . . . and one or two very small buildings of no value, in fact, none of them (has) any value today, for Yacolt is absolutely dead with no promise for a future life."

1932— The NP stopped its passenger service to Yacolt.

Turmoil, tumult and transition

1947-1958—A dizzying series of acquisitions, mergers and other developments characterized the local railroad and lumber scene. Historical sources vary on matters such as when a given lease, merger, dissolution or construction project was announced versus when it was completed or took effect. Here's the best we could establish for these 11 years:

1947-1948—Yacolt's status since 1903 as the terminus of the railroad, born in 1887, was ending. Harbor Plywood Co. of Hoquiam bought 28,000 acres of Northern Pacific Railway's Skamania County forest land and began building—or soon would—a 6.2-mile extension of the rail line from Yacolt to Chelatchie.

1950 —The Longview, Portland and Northern Railway (LP&N), a Kansas-based Long-Bell Lumber Co. subsidiary, acquired the new rail extension from Harbor Plywood and later bought the remainder of the line from the Northern Pacific.

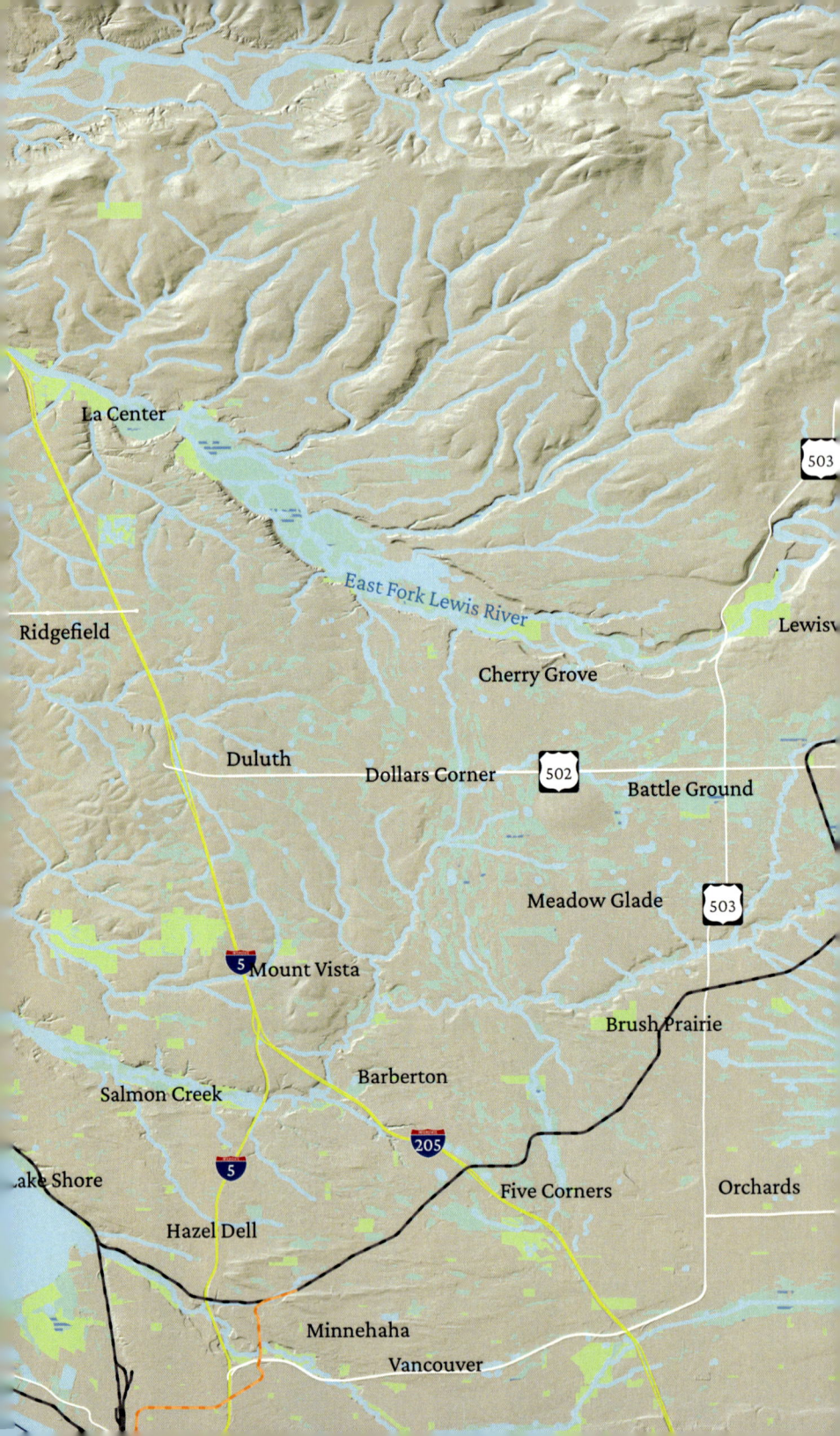

La Center

503

Ridgefield

East Fork Lewis River

Cherry Grove

Lewisv

Duluth

Dollars Corner

502

Battle Ground

Meadow Glade

503

5 Mount Vista

Brush Prairie

Salmon Creek

Barberton

205

ake Shore

5

Hazel Dell

Five Corners

Orchards

Minnehaha

Vancouver

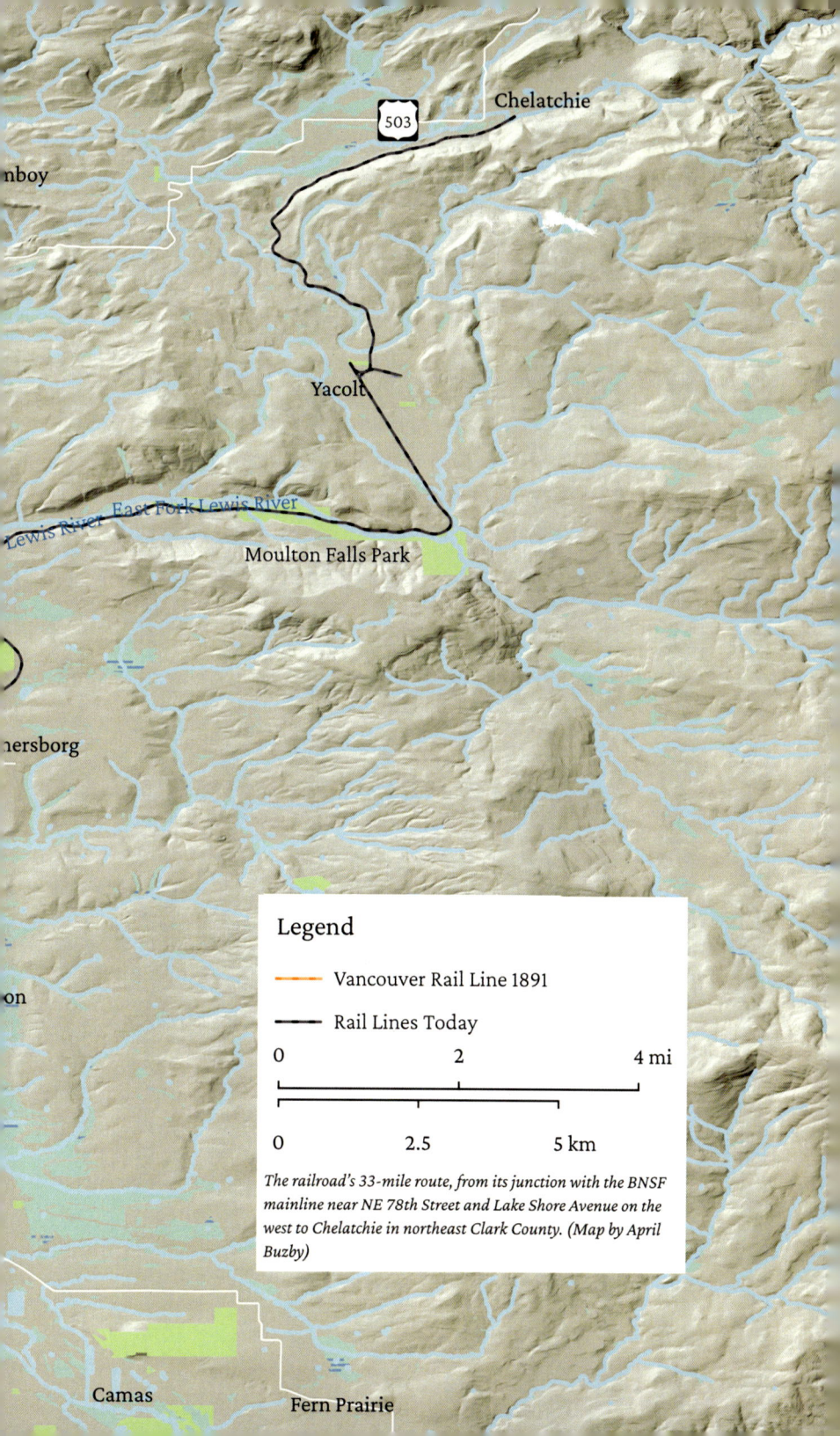

Chelatchie

503

Yacolt

East Fork Lewis River
Lewis River

Moulton Falls Park

Legend

⎯⎯ Vancouver Rail Line 1891

⎯⎯ Rail Lines Today

0   2   4 mi

0   2.5   5 km

The railroad's 33-mile route, from its junction with the BNSF mainline near NE 78th Street and Lake Shore Avenue on the west to Chelatchie in northeast Clark County. (Map by April Buzby)

1956—International Paper Co. (IP) merged with the Long-Bell Lumber Co. and its Longview subsidiary, the LP&N Railway. This merger gave IP control of the new Chelatchie-Yacolt line.

April 1960—International Paper Co., now owner of the LP&N, built a sprawling lumber and plywood plant in Chelatchie. It would employ as many as 600, counting lumberjacks and truck drivers. In addition, International Paper acquired from the Northern Pacific the 27-mile leg of the rail line from Yacolt to Rye near N.E. 68th Street and St. Johns Boulevard. Designated as the Chelatchie Division of the LP&N, it meant the end of the NP's day-to-day operations on the line after more than a half-century. But the NP still owned the remaining track from Rye to the Vancouver Junction at Lake Shore Avenue. A period of relative calm and stability prevailed over the Chelatchie mill and its railroad for almost two decades until...

Mill closes, railroad sold

June 30, 1979—International Paper Co. shut its Chelatchie plywood and lumber mill due at least partly to declining timber supplies. Traffic on the Chelatchie Division of the Longview, Portland & Northern Railway plummeted. In 1980 the line was put up for sale.

July 17, 1980—Vancouver businessmen Jerry Prom, Byron Slack, and Dave Callaham formed the Chelatchie Prairie Railroad Co. In March 1981 they purchased the 29.5-mile Chelatchie-Rye line from the Longview, Portland & Northern Railway for $450,000 and operated freight and some excursion service. Initially, the excursions were run by David Reed of Ridgefield under the name Chelatchie Prairie Train Rides Inc.

January 1984— The short-haul freight-railroad business didn't pan out. The owners sought and received permission from the federal Interstate Commerce Commission to discontinue service and abandon the line. Slack and Callaham wanted to sell the railroad to the county for $5.5 million.

County's goals

Four major arguments surfaced for the county to buy the line and thus ensure its future: (1) Spur economic growth near the tracks (construction, jobs, tax revenue); (2) encourage excursion trains as a local amenity and tourist attraction; (3) establish a 33-mile trail for hikers, bikers and horseback riders on or near the railroad right of way; (4) lock in the right of way in case it should someday be needed for utilities in the growing Vancouver metro area. Arguments against public ownership included cost to taxpayers, negative impact on adjacent property values and potential environmental harm resulting from development.

Summer 1986—The county began the process of buying the railroad and considering applicants to operate the line. Marvin Case, publisher of the weekly *Battle Ground Reflector*, saw the excursion railroad as a business opportunity that summer. He and a partner, Brooks Owen, worked out a short-term lease.

Case paid $100 per excursion to use facilities and equipment, including rolling stock. The two-hour trips ran from Battle Ground north, past the Heisson Store and along the East Fork of the Lewis River past Moulton Falls Park and back.

"The first day, we had 300 people lined up to ride," Case says. "We jammed 'em in" at $6 per adult. "*The Columbian* ran a front-page story, and that attracted more riders. It was a new thing, a big adventure. For Battle Ground, it was a big plus."

November 14, 1986—The county's purchase was finalized with the 3-0 vote of Clark Commissioners John McKibbin (D), Dave Sturdevant (D) and Vern Veysey (R). The deal included property, buildings and bridges, for $1,251,911. The name "Chelatchie Prairie Railroad" was gone, but not for long.

April 17, 1987—The Lewis & Clark Railway Co. (LINC), created by Northern Rail Services of Tacoma, was the next operator of freight service. Ed Berntsen, a former Northern Pacific and Burlington Northern telegrapher, freight agent, train dispatcher and transportation manager, was LINC's founder, president and general manager. Berntsen signed a seven-year lease with Clark County. A 10-year lease would follow.

Berntsen adopted a color scheme and logos reminiscent of the long-gone golden age of train travel across Washington state on the Northern Pacific, the Great Northern and the Spokane, Portland & Seattle railroads. The SP&S had become one of Clark County's largest employers, with a sprawling train assembly and repair yard, including roundhouse, in Fruit Valley.

May 1, 1987—LINC began freight service under a seven-year lease with the county. The lease would later be renewed for another 10 years.

Berntsen adopted a Northern Pacific color scheme and logos reminiscent of the glory days of train travel across Washington state on the Northern Pacific, the Great Northern and the Spokane, Portland & Seattle railroads. (The SP&S was one of Clark County's largest employers, with a sprawling train switch yard and repair shops, including roundhouse, in Fruit Valley.)

June 6, 1987—LINC began spring-to-fall passenger excursions between Battle Ground and Moulton Falls County Park but those ended about 1994. A popular annual Christmas tree-gathering excursion train ran for a few more years.

Cross-county trail envisioned

In 1988 county commissioners took a step toward creating the proposed 33-mile trail alongside or near the tracks by approving a Chelatchie Prairie Rail with Trail Study. Note the "with." Commissioners were not proposing a trail to replace tracks.

February 1996—A washout under the track next to the Bonneville Power Administration's Ross Complex in Hazel Dell closed the entire line for a year. During the closure LINC continued serving its customers by transferring freight by truck to the main line. The BNSF that year donated to the county the last privately owned stretch of the historic line, 3.62 miles from Rye to Vancouver Junction.

Freight cars handled by Portland Vancouver Junction Railroad wait for connection to BNSF mainline near Burnt Bridge Creek. (Photo by author)

1998—The all-volunteer Battle Ground, Yacolt & Chelatchie Prairie Railroad Association (BYCX.org) was formed with the goal of restoring the deteriorating line in north county for excursion service. Commonly known as the Chelatchie Prairie Railroad, it has free use of the county-owned line but is responsible for maintaining the tracks except at crossings and bridges. It owns and maintains its rolling stock.

"We love our trains and want to provide education and entertainment to the citizens of Southwest Washington," says Doug Auburg, treasurer of the BYCX. "Volunteers are always welcome to help with everything from selling tickets to equipment maintenance, with on-the-job training for skilled positions.

May 26, 2001—Excursions were reinstated on the northern end of the line. In the summer of 2023 we took the 10 mph, 14-mile round trip between Yacolt and Moulton Station on the East Fork of the Lewis River. The outing included the 342-foot tunnel, the 522-foot bridge over the river (163-foot steel span plus approaches) and a 30-minute stop to allow for a short walk to check out Yacolt Falls. At this writing, volunteers continue work on upgrading tracks elsewhere between Heisson and Chelatchie with federal and state financial help in 2022 and 2023.

2004, freight service—The line was leased to Columbia Basin Railroad of the Moses Lake-Othello area in Eastern Washington, owned by the Temple Family. Eric Temple owns the Portland Vancouver Junction Railroad (PVJR) and operates from Battle Ground to the main line at Vancouver Junction.

Trail in limbo

2005—The county received a $230,000 federal transportation enhancement grant for a Chelatchie Prairie Rail with Trail Corridor Study.

July 2008—County commissioners approved the plan for the hiking, biking and equestrian trail. The Columbian reported the plan was to link 22.5 miles of new trails to 6.5

Excursion train from Yacolt approaches Lucia Falls Road just before crossing East Fork of the Lewis River. (Photo by author)

miles of existing trails (Burnt Bridge Creek, Padden Parkway and Moulton Falls Regional Park) and four miles of roadway improvements.

December 2011—The first section of newly built trail over the 33-mile route opened. The paved segment runs from the entrance of Battle Ground State Park southwest along the tracks to near N.E. 167th Avenue and N.E. 231st Street.

Now what?—As of summer 2023, the dream of a cross-county trail existed in the form of the 2008 study collecting dust on shelves in county offices. No other new segment was in the works or planning stages. The county's railroad coordinator, Kevin Tyler, told us "There are no current prospects for more trails."

Lease dispute settled

Dueling lawsuits in 2022 between Clark County and PVJR had cast a shadow over their relationship and the county's long-range plans and hopes for the line. But by June 2023, the relationship appeared to be back on solid footing.

Chelatchie Prairie Railroad excursion train on a summer 2023 run. (Photo by author)

Kevin Tyler, the county's railroad coordinator, said, "The county settled a dispute and entered into a new lease agreement." The PVJR pays nothing to the county on the first 500 cars it moves in a given year. It pays the county $10 per carload from 501 to 1,500 cars in a year and $20 a carload for more than 1,500. In 2022 the PVJR line moved 795 cars.

Under the agreement, signed in December 2022, the PVJR leases from Clark County the entire 33.1 miles of the railroad, from its connection to the BNSF main line on Lake Shore Avenue to Chelatchie in northeast Clark County. The PVJR leases back to the county, the northernmost 18.7 miles of the line, from near the Heisson Store to Chelatchie. The county then subleases that stretch to the volunteer-operated Battle Ground, Yacolt, Chelatchie Prairie Railroad (BYCX) excursion line.

Development, conservation or both?

In the spring of 2023, as this article was being written for fall 2023 publication, *The Columbian* reported the potential for attracting new rail-dependent businesses along the line was "back on track."

The May 13 page 1 story began, "After a nearly five-year hiatus due to litigation, the Clark County Council is resuming plans to allow more development to utilize its short-line railroad (by moving) forward with rail-dependent industrial development on rural resource land adjacent to railroads."

But a week later, following a May 17 county council meeting, it seemed development prospects were still off the rails. *The Columbian* story began, "The question of how lands adjacent to Clark County's short-line railroad can be developed and used won't be easy to answer."

A immediate issue appears to be whether a 2017 state law allows for the extension of sewer lines outside the county's Growth Management Area. Such extensions, says Temple of the PVJR, are necessary to attract development, which presumably would mean more construction, jobs, taxes—and environmental impact—near the tracks.

What seemed clear in the summer of 2023 was the lack of clarity in the 2017 law. Clark County Councilor Gary Medvigy, for one, said in order to avoid another lawsuit the county should work with state lawmakers to clarify the law during the next legislative session.

Principal players in this saga have been Eric Temple, owner of the PVJR, Friends of Clark County (friendsofclarkcounty.org) and the Clark County Council.

Temple, who took over the freight-hauling railroad business on the county-owned tracks in 2004, is frustrated and frank about the issue. In a May 11 phone interview from his home in Medina, near Seattle, he said, "It is absolutely the biggest problem for this railroad. I've been promoting dual use for 20 years—recreation and business. The elected leaders have tilted strongly for pro-growth economic development. Then we have the unelected county staff, which is more pro-recreation. It's nuts. We've had many businesses that want to locate here but have been scared off by the staff."

Those fearful of sewer extensions include County Councilor Sue Marshall, a former Friends of Clark County board president. She is among those who say extending sewers would lead to

The Chelatchie Prairie Railroad's locomotive — a 1941 ALCO S-2 diesel switch engine — pushes the excursion train onto the 163-foot steel span over the East Fork of the Lewis River. From here, it's another one and a half miles to the end of the 5-mile route from Yacolt. On the return, the locomotive will be in front, pulling. At left is part of automatic lights and gate that stop traffic on Lucia Falls Road during crossings. (Photo by author)

urban sprawl, loss of agricultural land, scars on the landscape and heavy truck traffic on quiet county roads.

Then, in October 2023, another development surfaced in the increasingly bitter construction versus conservation battle. Residents complained that Chelatchie Creek was drying up and hundreds of fish had died as a result of the Portland Vancouver Junction Railroad's construction of a road over private property without the necessary approval from various government agencies. Temple was quoted in *The Columbian* responding, "Essentially, there are no permits required."

The Chelatchie Prairie Railroad, as it is popularly known, was born in 1887 as the Vancouver, Klickitat & Yakima Railroad by a dozen well-heeled Vancouver businessmen and political leaders with no railroad expertise or experience. They had a goal they could not achieve: crossing the Cascades by train. Now, as a county-owned entity, it faces another, arguably more complex, goal: Encouraging and facilitating economic development while creating a delightful, mostly rural, cross-county trail, all within reasonable and enforceable environmental guardrails.

Gregg Herrington, a Vancouver native who graduated from Clark College and the University of Washington, is retired after a 41-year career with The Oregonian, The Associated Press, and The Columbian.

WITH GRATITUDE

The author could not have written the complex 136-year history of today's Chelatchie Prairie Railroad—originally the Vancouver, Klickitat & Yakima Railroad —without the help of numerous resourceful fans of Northwest history, railroads and geography. Every person and organization named here contributed information and encouragement over the course of this nine-month project.

I owe an extra "Thank you" to these eight people who repeatedly filled in blanks, clarified the unclear, connected dots and supplied new information: Don Higgins, a Battle Ground historian and author; Doug Auburg of the all-volunteer Battle Ground, Yacolt & Chelatchie Prairie excursion railroad (BGYX); Karen Kettenring Caplinger of Battle Ground, who was repeatedly generous with her time and family history; Kevin Tyler, Clark County's railroad coordinator; the Grande Dames of Clark County history, Louise McKay Allworth Tucker of Battle Ground and Pat Jollota of Vancouver; Allen Thomas, retired Columbian outdoors writer who knows Gifford Pinchot National Forest geography like the back of his hand, and Edward Berntsen of Gig Harbor, Wash., a fountain of knowledge about Northwest railroad history with an inexhaustible enthusiasm for sharing it.

Others who provided information for this saga included: Lori Hidden Novak; Jerry Olson; Vincent Roman; Ceci Ryan Smith; City of Vancouver records specialist Matt Oftedahl; Yacolt Town Clerk Stephanie Fields; Sarah Dana and Lupita Lopez of the Washington State Archives office; the Denver office of the U.S. Geological Survey; Pacific Northwest Railroad Archives, in Burien Wash; Manistee, County, Mich., Historical Museum; Manistee County Library; Minnesota Historical Society; Minnesota State Archives; Northern Pacific Railway Historical Association; Great Northern Railway Historical Society; Gayle, O'Hara of WSU Archives; Eric Temple of the Portland Vancouver Junction Railroad; Bob Weaver of the Pacific Northwest Chapter, National Railway Historical Society; Tom Gronewald, Vancouver; Paul D. Curtiss, Tacoma; John Boule, Yakima County Historical Museum; Doug Shearer, Northern Pacific Railway Museum, Toppenish Wash.; Jerry Dean and Laurene Eldred, Glenwood Wash.; Cheryl Mack and Rick McClure, Trout Lake, Wash.; Dan Cozine, Bothell Wash.; David Sprau, St. Helens Ore.; Katie Bush, and April Buzby, Clark County Historical Museum; Martin Middlewood, Clark County Historical Society and editor of this book; and the late Carl Landerholm, whose 1960 "Vancouver Area Chronology" from 1784 to 1958 is an absolute treasure.

Do Everything: The WCTU in SW Washington

Agitate, educate, and organize were its watchwords

Tracy Reilly Kelly

E verything is not in the temperance reform, but the temperance reform should be in everything." Frances Willard

On July 10, 1883, the "most famous woman in America," Frances Willard, arrived by ferry in Vancouver. President of the Women's Christian Temperance Movement (WCTU), no stop was too small for her ambitious western tour called the Crusade Roundup. (Hodge Evans, pp. 146-147) Thousands attended her speech in Portland in June 1883. (Soden, 199) With her electrifying presence, she would "re-christen" the membership of the WCTU chapter in Vancouver, originally formed in 1877. ("Women's Christian") Brought in by members of the First Methodist Church, she spoke to a large audience at Marsh's Hall after speaking to the Vancouver Barracks in the afternoon. *The Vancouver Independent*, on July 12, 1883, said of her speech,

> She is an eloquent speaker and the most rational person on the temperance issue we ever listened to, her ideas being void of the extreme radical notions of most temperance people.

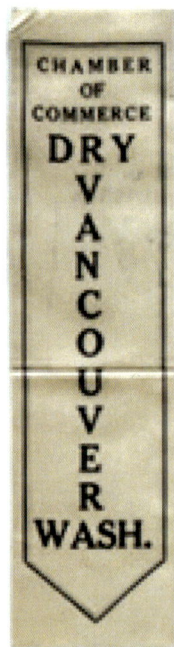

Chamber of Commerce Dry Ribbon, date unknown (Source: CCHM archive)

In 1879, the WCTU elected Frances Willard as its second president. A Methodist, Willard was an academic with a genius for organizing. (Hodge Evans, 193) Her vision was to expand the WCTU's methods and its program for reform into executing more overtly political actions. Not content with just moral persuasion toward an abstinent society, Willard advocated for wide social reforms. She realized that no significant political change that women desired could occur without the vote. Woman suffrage became the cornerstone of the priorities. Calling her new platform the "Do Everything" program, Willard sought to—do everything. (Willard, 90 – 170)

She galvanized one of the largest women's organizations in the world, mobilizing thousands of women working together to get outside of their homes to bring the "heaven on earth" that Willard promised. The WCTU created "departments," or administrative units. By 1896, 25 of the 39 dealt with non-temperance social justice issues.

Out of this same First Methodist Church, the Clarke County Equal Rights Association (CCERA) was formed in the next year, 1884, with the object, "The encouragement and assistance of women in the exercise of the right of suffrage and for other purposes." ("Equal Rights Association") Clearly, under the thrall of Willard's "Do Everything" program, gaining suffrage for Clark County women was crucial to temperance. Once women could vote, purer virtues would come to dominate the laws of the state and nation.

Frances Willard (Source: US Library of Congress's Prints and Photographs division ppmsc.00035)

Dr. Ella Whipple, WCTU superintendent influencing the press, was also the CCERA secretary. WCTU Board members were among the 31 signers to the equal rights formation. Suffrage legislation did pass temporarily in the territory but was not instituted at statehood in 1889.

Temperance was a huge force in Washington since its territorial days. Even before the rest of the nation, the state made the prohibition of alcohol the law of the land beginning in 1916. (Becker, "Prohibition") No group was more exultant under this ruling than the WCTU. They had won the hard fight, and the nation's very core would be saved from the ruination of "demon rum." (Hodge, 318) Even if, for only a period of time.

Dr. Ella Whipple. (Source: Willard, Frances E. A woman of the century; fourteen hundred-seventy biographical sketches accompanied by portraits of leading American women in all walks of life. Buffalo, New York, Charles Wells Moulton, 1893. PDF.)

Many observers have tied women's attempts to gain suffrage—the right to vote—to the issue of temperance. Were these two political movements allied? Are temperance and prohibition the same concept, or are there differences within these approaches?

Temperance is a term denoting actions that have a quality of moderation or self-restraint, it involves usage in many other forms than just alcohol. Early reformers wanted just this—self-restraint in consumption rather than prohibition. (Becker, "Prohibition") Temperance reformers were called "templars." Initiated by the Legislature in 1923, today, Washington State students still celebrate Temperance and Good Citizenship on January 16.

Prohibition means forbidding something entirely, especially by law. As the Women's Christian Temperance Union gained in institutional strength, it became centered on the larger task of prohibition. A national Prohibition Party began in 1869, with WCTU support. And, in 1900, two percent of Washington voters cast their ballots for this party. In 1912, it was three percent of voters. (Becker, "Prohibition")

Alcohol use in the 19th century was very different than what we know today. Most Americans, including children, drank alcoholic beverages like weak beer daily. Water was unsafe to drink throughout most of human history, and alcohol kills harmful bacteria. Paul Vallee, in Scientific American states.

...through Western history, the normal state of mind may have been one of inebriation. In a world of contaminated and dangerous water supplies, alcohol truly earned the

Local Gathering of the Women's Christian Temperance Union (Source: Clark County Historical Museum cchm04662)

title granted to it in the Middle
Ages, aqua vitae, the water of life.
(Vallee, "Conflicted History")

What could be an average level
of insobriety could rapidly change
into venal, violent drunkenness.
Women knew this. If it had not
happened to her family personally,

WCTU Logo

she surely saw it in her neighborhood. She had sat with other
women in countless commiserations. It was common to know
men who drank their entire wages, leaving nothing for food
or sustenance. Fathers worried that their inheritance to their
beloved adult daughters would be destroyed by alcoholic bad
decisions by their sons-in-law. Fortunes were lost. The over-
the-top language used by temperance advocates had deep
resonance for women harmed by the overuse of alcoholic spirits.
(Willard, 35-49) If women suffered at the hands of abusive
husbands, they could not speak about it directly. Yet, they could
speak about it indirectly by raising their voices together, in
unity, against alcoholism and what alcohol does to men.

The WCTU was founded in Cleveland, Ohio in 1874. Early
on, women would go to saloons and fall down on their knees to
pray. This successful campaign had results—women crusaded
in more than 900 communities with many going dry .(often
temporarily so) Saloons were not only recreational gathering
places but many American political meetings were also held
in saloons. (Frances Willard House, "History WCTU") In
contentious election news coverage, the *Vancouver Weekly
Columbian*, on Oct 28, 1892, accuses "every man who pretended
to be a voter being marched from the saloon to the primary."
("Ring Politics")

The WCTU watchwords were "Agitate – Educate –
Organize." But to allow women to get out into the public and,
moreover, speak in public, cultural mores would need to change.

What better way to do this than to extend the protection of the home to women doing justice work outside of the home? "Home Protection" became the motto of the WCTU. This battle was one for the very preservation and purity of children, family and of course, religion. (Hodge, 3, 31, 143)

Local chapters were called "Unions" and were largely autonomous. In Clark County, there were Central and East unions and very powerful Camas, Battle Ground and Woodland unions. State and national headquarters linked them. There were clear channels for authority. The white ribbon bow was adopted, emblematically symbolizing purity. Through education and example, women could make the change in the world that she wanted to see. (Willard, 51-103) In progressive Vancouver, taking up the "Do Everything" concept would revitalize the chapter. News is related through the newspapers —and the churches.

After Willard's usual electrifying July 1883 visit, a strong local union of 30 members was formed. ("Vancouver W.C.T.U. Founder") The new union chapter was called the Willard Chapter. The following officers were elected: President Mrs. S.R. Whipple; vice presidents Mrs. Mary Blake, Mrs. Gertrude Evans, Mrs. E.J. Troup and Miss Lucy Brewster; recording secretary, Mrs. Margaret Jaggy; corresponding secretary, Mrs. Rebecca Brown; treasurer Miss Dena Wintler; superintendent educational work Mrs. L.G. Bell; superintendent Sunday school work, Mrs. H.H. Gridley; Superintendent juvenile work Miss Agnes Epert; superintendent temperance literature Mrs. H.A. Morrow; superintendent among the soldiers Mrs. Elizabeth Durgin; superintendent influencing the press, Dr. Ella Whipple. ("W.C.T.U") These women represented Vancouver's wealth and class, families that had crossed the plains.

A committed temperance and suffrage worker, Ella Whipple occupied nearly all the high and responsible positions in the Vancouver chapter of the Woman's Christian Temperance Association and at the Methodist Episcopal Church. Dr.

Whipple held myriad community roles. Not just a physician, she was also superintendent of schools. Ella was twice a delegate to the Territorial Republican convention in 1884 and in 1886. At great loss to Vancouver's "Do Everything" women's stewardship, Dr. Whipple moved to Pasadena, CA, where she continued as a notable temperance leader. (Livermore, 755-756)

In Washington state, Seattle hosted one of the few Black WCTU chapters, founded by suffrage pioneer Frances Ellen Watkins Harper. The Frances Harper Union was hosted by the First African Methodist Episcopal Church. (Andrews, "Women's Christian") Harper had established a number of "Colored Section" WCTU unions across the country, and the organization was unique in forming these. But Willard's vision was a separatist one. In the 1890's Black journalist Ida B. Wells would very publicly accuse the WCTU of appeasing Southern Jim Crow racism and taking no stance against lynching. Harper became disillusioned at the racist actions that kept Black unions in a secondary position, in segregated groups with no access to power centers or decisions. (Hodge, 188-189; 274-286) While receiving high marks from the Western Washington WCTU, the Harper Union in Seattle disbanded at the request of First African Church, which would go on to host their own group. (Andrews, "Women's Christian")

For Vancouver's white, privileged women, the WCTU's Protestant ideals fit in neatly. The slogan "For God and Home and Native Land" emphasizes the concept called Nativism. This was an attempt to control immigration using fears and stereotypes by the white middle and upper class. Large percentages of new immigrants to the U.S. in the late 19th century came from Italy and the Baden-Wurttemberg and Bavarian regions of southern Germany. These regions had large Catholic populations, and immigration problems became identified with Catholicism. They also had traditions of consuming spirits. (Jaret, 1-13; 24) Vancouver, site of the US Army Barracks and multiple breweries, had established itself as a "wet" town early on. There was a strong liquor lobby. The WCTU denounced recent immigrants by linking them with heavy drinking—Italians with wine, Germans with beer. A venal nativism fed into these tropes. Native land was later changed to "Every Land" in the slogan when the WCTU became world-wide.

In early 1890, a formidable new advocate appeared in Vancouver—Maria Louisa Trenholm Hidden. Married to Jackson Hidden, a later son of one of Vancouver's entrepreneurial Hidden family, Maria L.T. was president of the Vermont Woman Suffrage Association before moving west and, in 1884, had served as superintendent of the "Sabbath Schoolwork" department of the WCTU in Vermont. (Kanell, 1-2) She was an experienced campaigner.

Hidden began to lead clubs in Vancouver soon after her arrival. She was local president of the Vancouver WCTU—and vice president and superintendent of Sunday School Work of the Washington state WCTU. Hidden would write a monthly column on Fridays for the *Vancouver Weekly Columbian* beginning in 1890 and going for a decade. Titled "W.C.T.U. Column," with the banner "*For God, Home and Native Land*," Maria would write about WCTU meetings, conventions and Portland and national news. ("W.C.T.U. Column") In one romantically inspired column on Aug 31, 1894, she described the coastal beauty and scenery she encountered at a large camp meeting and listed the new officers. She was president, and Mrs. A Peebles vice president, corresponding secretary was Mrs. Pearl Rollins, recording secretary, Mrs. L.N. Wisnall, and treasurer, Miss Augusta Christ.

Hidden appeared to be a magnet for negative attention. In her *Columbian* column of June 22, 1894, she bitterly states that she must defend herself in the public press for the first time! Her column described being attacked in the newspaper, which reported that the "Vancouver union had recently disavowed the column" – but this was not true! She also went to great lengths to discuss that she had not kept funds intended for the state convention. On June 26 in a front-page article saying "Mrs. Hidden in Self Defense," WCTU members send in a petition accompanying her letter accusing "Vancouver businessmen" of lying, stating she was rejected for membership in the Taxpayers League—and this erroneous news reached the state convention, smearing her righteous name.

Hidden was a leader of "second generation feminists" who famously did battle with Abigail Scott Duniway. (Madden, "Esther Pohl,") Duniway, the leading suffragist in the entire Pacific Northwest and a friend and collaborator of Susan B. Anthony, opposed temperance. She felt that it was a barrier to suffrage and alienated the very men needed to vote yes to women voting. (Duniway, "Ballots and Bullets") M.L.T. Hidden made direct charges against Duniway in at least two instances. In one, covered by the *Vancouver Independent* in April 1895, local women in a suffragist club nationally conceived by Anthony called Wimodausis (Wives, mothers, daughters, sisters), 17 out of 19 members handed in their resignations and marched out as a body because Duniway was the featured speaker. Hidden then led these women to form a new Ladies Athenaeum club. (Gaston, 604; "Maria L.T.") In 1905, she made direct negative accusations against Duniway at a Portland meeting attended by Vancouver leaders organizing the National American Women's Suffrage Association national convention.

Vancouver proved to be too backwater for Maria and Jackson Hidden. They moved to Portland in 1900, where he became a successful businessman. She went to Portland to be a WCTU leader—and to unsuccessfully run for various political offices. (Gaston, 604)

The campaign for state prohibition heated up in the early 20th century. A local law option for prohibition had been available to individual towns since its passage in 1909. Communities could hold a vote to ban local sales. Vancouver and Camas would remain "wet," Washougal "dry," but in

Southwest Washington, prohibition messages were gaining ground, and these votes might switch yearly. ("Vancouver Wet") On November 3, 1914, after prodigious effort by coordinated groups, Washington Initiative 3 was passed, statewide 189,840 to 171,204. This statutory law, not a constitutional amendment, prohibited the production and distribution of alcohol. It did not ban consumption. Rural votes won against cities like Seattle, Spokane and Tacoma. It would be a year later, on Dec 31, 1915, that the law would take effect. One could import 12 quarts of beer or two quarts of hard liquor every 20 days. This led to a widespread illegal sales market. Pharmacies cropped up immediately, a source for underground sales, 65 in Seattle in 1916 alone. (Becker, "Prohibition")

Four years later, in 1917, Congress passed the 18th Amendment, also known as the Volstead Act. Washington would be the 22nd state to ratify—unanimously in both House and Senate, on January 13, 1919.

While the Vancouver WCTU gave a copy of Anna Gordon's "Life of Frances Willard" to the Vancouver Library in 1918, and they supported a French war orphan ("W.C.T.U. Will"), the lofty ideals of "Do Everything" had been largely discarded nationwide in the decades after Willard's death in 1898. ("Temperance, Feminism") While the WCTU had laid the foundation for the women's movements that followed by enabling women's empowerment, things were changing for American women. Rights were being awarded and freedoms gained.

After the successes of gaining the vote and national Prohibition, the fight had tapered off in Clark County after 1916. Now focusing just on supporting a prohibitionist society, the "New Woman" of the early 1900s, who sought to be free of the stultifying cult of the "Ideal of Real Womanhood," would become the Jazz Age flapper of the 1920s. More intent on personal and sexual freedom, and rejecting Victorian mores, women began to take charge of their own lives. ("Women,

Temperance") New organizations in Vancouver, like the League of Women Voters in September 1920 and the Young Women's Christian Association (YWCA) in 1916, were more in line with women engaged in political life. In Clark County, women, like Elizabeth Crawford Sterling, who would founded the local branch of the American Association of University Women in 1931, and May Haack ran for office—and were elected. Ruth Karr McKee, a University of Washington regent, commandeered the General Women's Club and the League of Women Voters to hold citizenship classes and look at issues like women's incarceration and marriage equality. ("Make Marriage Laws") The YWCA founded a lunch counter at 513 ½ Main Street to aid working women.

In SW Washington, the WCTU in the 1920s and 30s reflected these transformations. It began to have a reputation as full of teetotaling moral zealots. Woman appealed to one set of the population while repelling the other. Like WCTU women in other states, they became more conservative, focusing on evangelical Christianity, and less involved in social justice. (Toast to Misunderstood;" McArthur, "Women's Christian")

The Columbian reported monthly WCTU activities throughout in the 1920s. Membership was strong enough to hold events. An oratorical contest and a school essay contest on the values of temperance were held yearly. A strong emphasis on anti-smoking and anti-narcotics joined the anti-liquor crusade. War orphans were supported. Yet some of these activities revealed a darker side to the organization in the 1920s.

In the Northwest, the WCTU had joined forces with the Anti-Saloon League in the 1920s to "finish the business of Prohibition" and get rid of moonshine production. In 1923, National lecturer Mrs. Jackson Stilbaugh of Seattle cited *The Unfinished Task*" of national submission at a large Northwest convention where both groups shared the lectern. National organizer Louise Hollister toured Vancouver in her quest for one million members. ("Enforced Law Demand") On Dec. 29, 1923,

WCTU ladies joyfully watched "Sheriffs Let Booze Run Down to the Sea" reporting on a enormous dumping of illegal liquor. Rev. Charles C. Curtis arrived in the early 1920s to become pastor at the First Christian Church. Curtis traveled the state lecturing to mass meeting audiences as large as 2,000 on the subject of "America for Americans." His wife, Ethel, would be a WCTU chapter leader and delegate to the state convention in 1923. ("Personals") In Dec. 1921, Curtis gave the devotional to the WCTU December meeting. ("Central W.C.T.U Give") Rev C.C. Curtis was also the Grand Dragon of the Ku Klux Klan. (Middlewood, "Charles Cecil") He was a member of the Anti-Saloon League, whose membership included other Ku Klux Klan members. (Hansen, "KKK and WCTU") The revitalized nativist Klan, partnering with the Anti-Saloon League, had a period of immense popularity in the early 1920s and associated itself with the campaign against Catholics, immigrants and drinking. Polk's Directory listed the Klan with other fraternities. In SW Washington, the Klan held large rallies and picnics— thousands at Bagley Park. ("Klan will Stage") A large women's contingent was part of the organization.

However, the most excitement caused by the WCTU in the 1920's itself occurred in May 1926. The presidents of both Central and East Vancouver unions, Mrs. Charles Brown and Mrs. Arnold, presented a resolution to the Vancouver City Council deploring the use of a city building to serve alcohol. At the apex of prohibition, the charge spattered across *The Columbian* headline declaring that intoxicating beverages were served at a Smith-Reynolds American Legion banquet, held at the city's Memorial Hall, in violation of the 18th amendment. These allegations were taken very seriously. Councilman A. J. Collings investigated the charges, but no actions were taken. Many city leaders were at the dinner, including Mayor Storey, Chief of Police Crite and Clark County Sheriff Thompson. All leaders testified that they saw no alcohol consumption, with particular fervor by Sheriff Thompson. They did acknowledge there was a possibility of behind-the-scenes flask consumption. ("Denials Mark")

Washington State followed its progressive reputation and ended prohibition earlier than the U.S. did nationally. In January 1932, State Initiative 61 repealed all of Washington's liquor laws except the sales to minors, passing by a 61% margin on November 8 that year. (Becker, "Prohibition") Local federal legislators were sent the message to go to D.C. and help repeal the Volstead Act in March 1933. The local WCTU in Clark County lasted until the 1950s. Although usually characterized as a conservative movement, much of the enthusiasm that drove the early campaign for prohibition in Clark County was generated by progressive reformers, followers of Frances Willard. They saw the elimination of alcohol as a pathway for a better world. But Prohibition highlighted a range of problems that these women had not foreseen or able to admit. These included problems with legal enforcement, but much worse by waves of organized crime. It raised civil liberties questions—to what extent does anyone have the right to consume substances harmful to their body? These tensions between personal liberties and responsibilities to one's community continue to be major issues locally, and in the United States.

Tracy Reilly Kelly semi-retired as Program Manager and Instructor at Clark College. Tracy received her B.A. in Human Services from Evergreen State College and an M.S.T. in Health Education at Portland State University. She teaches history courses at Clark, and volunteers for the Clark County Historical Museum. Tracy was an author and curator of the HerStory exhibit. An avid genealogist, she is writing a book on her search for her family ancestors.

Works Cited

Andrews, Mildred, "Women's Christian Temperance Union, Western Washington." *History Link*, Dec. 2, 1998. www.historylink.org/file/407

Becker, Paula, "Prohibition in Washington State," *History Link*, Nov 20, 2010. www.historylink.org/file/9630

"Central W.C.T.U to Give Program," *Columbian*, Dec. 9, 1921, p.1.

"Denials Mark Legion Post Banquet Liquor Inquiry," *Columbian*, May 19, 1926, p.1.

Duniway, Abigail Scott, "Ballots and Bullets," Jan. 1889, *She Flies with Her Own Wings: The Collected Speeches of Abigail Scott Duniway,*" AS Duniway. org. asduniway.org/%E2%80%9Cballots-and-bullets%E2%80%9D-circa-january-21-23-1889/

"Enforced Law is Demand of the People," *Statesman Journal* (Salem, Oregon) Wed, Apr 11, 1923, p. 1.

"Equal Rights Association," *Vancouver Independent*, Feb 21, 1884, p. 5.

Gaston, Joseph. *Portland Oregon, It's History and Builders, The Benefactors, The Literary People, the Poets and Historians.* Wikisource. 1911, Vol.1. pg. 604. en.wikisource.org/wiki/Portland,_Oregon:_Its_History_and_Builders/ Volume_1/Chapter_29

Hansen, David, "KKK and WCTU: Partners in Prohibition," *Leben, A Journal for Reformation Life*, July 20, 2012. leben.us/kkk-wctu-partners-prohibition/

Hardy, Sarah B, "Temperance and Beyond: The Oregon Women's Temperance Union and Progressive Reform During the First World War," Senior seminar, Western Oregon University May 25, 2010. pp. 4-7.

Hodge Evans, Christopher. *Do Everything – The Biography of Frances Willard.* Oxford: Oxford University Press, 2022, pp. 3, 31, 143, 146-147; 188-189; 193; 274-286, 318.

Jaret, Charles., "Troubled by Newcomers: Anti-Immigrant Attitudes and Actions During Two Eras of Mass Immigration to the United States," *Journal of Ethnic American History*, Vol. 18, No. 3, Champaign: University of Illinois Press, 1999, pp. 11-13; 24.

"Klan will Stage Huge Ceremonial Here on Aug. 23," *Columbian*, Aug 8, 1924, p.1.

Livermore, Mary. *Willard, Frances. A Woman of the Century: Fourteen Hundred-seventy biographical sketches.* Cambridge: Harvard University, 1893, p.755.

Madden, Sara, "Esther Pohl Lovejoy and Prohibition, 1920," Oregon Women's History Consortium. www.oregonwomenshistory.org/ dr-esther-pohl-lovejoy-and-prohibition-1920-by-sara-madden/

"Make Marriage Laws More Uniform," *Columbian* Jan 30, 1924, p.1.

"Maria L. T. Hidden,' *The Oregon Daily Journal*, May 2, 1920, p. 20.

McArthur, Judith N, "Women's Christian Temperance Union," Texas State Historical Association, April 1, 2001. www.tshaonline.org/handbook/ entries/womans-christian-temperance-union.

Middlewood, Martin, "Clark County History: Charles Cecil Curtis, Grand Dragon of Washington," *Columbian*, Aug 23, 2020. https://www.columbian.com/news/2020/aug/23/ clark-county-history-charles-cecil-curtis-grand-dragon-of-washington/

Morrison, Pat, "A Toast to the Misunderstood Temperance Movement on the Anniversary of its Demise," *Los Angeles Times*, Dec 6, 2022. www.latimes.com/california/

story/2022-12-06/a-toast-to-the-misunderstood-temperance-movement-on-the-anniversary-of-its-demise

"Mrs. Hidden in Self Defense," *Vancouver Weekly Columbian*, Jun 26, 1894, p.4.

"Personals," *Columbian*, Oct 9, 1923, p.2.

"Ring Politics," *Vancouver Weekly Columbian*, Oct 28, 1892, p.2.

"Sheriff Lets Booze Go Down to the Sea," *Columbian*, Dec 29, 1921, p.1.

Tyrrell, Ian, "Temperance, Feminism, and the WCTU: New Interpretations and New Directions," Australasian Journal of American Studies, Vol 5, No 2, Dec. 1986, pp.27-32.

www.jstor.org/stable/41053417 pp27-32

Vallee, Paul, "The Conflicted History of Alcohol in Western Civilization," *Scientific American*, June 1, 2015. www.scientificamerican.com/article/the-conflicted-history-of-alcohol-in-western-civilization/

"Vancouver W.C.T.U. Founded in 1883 by Willard," *Columbian*, Feb 23, 1923, p.1.

"Vancouver Wet by Majority of 136," *Vancouver Weekly Columbian*, Nov 4, 1909, p.1.

"W.C.T.U.," *Vancouver Independent*, Jul 12, 1883, p.5.

"W.C.T.U. Column," Maria L. T. Hidden, *Vancouver Weekly Columbian*, Dec. 17, 1890, p.1.

"W.C.T.U. Column," Maria L. T. Hidden, *Vancouver Weekly Columbian*, July 17, 1891, p.1.

"W.C.T.U. Column," Maria L. T. Hidden, *Vancouver Weekly Columbian*, June 22, 1894, p.3.

"W.C.T.U. Column," Maria L. T. Hidden, *Vancouver Weekly Columbian*, Aug 31, 1894, p.2.

"W.C.T.U. Organizer Will Make Tour of County Soon," *Columbian*, April 6, 1921, p. 1.

"W.C.T.U. Will Support French War Orphan," *Columbian*, Jan. 24, 1918, p. 1.

Willard, Frances. *Do Everything: A Handbook for World's White Ribboner.* Chicago: The Women's Temperance Publishing Association, 1895. pp.35-49; 90 – 170.

"Women's Christian Temperance Union Formed," *Vancouver Independent*, Feb. 2, 1877, p.4.

Perils of an Airborne Wedding

When balloons couldn't work, a youth's flightless airplane did

Martin Middlewood

L ife in local communities makes curious intersections, sometimes at the county fair. Weddings mixed with aviation in Vancouver made news throughout Washington State for months in 1911, causing confusion on several levels, process, legal and practical—ending at the Clark County Harvest Days (the fair name that year). The Henry Claussen-Nina Stanley wedding announcement didn't seem anything more than ordinary. The bride had it printed tasteful, although in a torturous hard-to-read Germanic script reminiscent of the *Guttenberg Bible*. Unraveling the script, the reader finds Henry H. Claussen and Nina C. Stanley would marry in Vancouver on Saturday, October 17. Nice, but not impressive. Obviously, this is but one of many ordinary nuptials that year. Then the eye catches the smaller, easy-to-read modern print in all capitals at the lower left-hand corner declaring:

**AN AVIATION WEDDING
1000 FEET ABOVE
THE EARTH**

In the early days of aviation, this was the equivalent of getting married during a Superbowl half-time today. Arranging either would be attention-getting, costly and difficult to negotiate. Nothing is mentioned about where the pair might lift aloft from—or in what. At the time, the Vancouver Barracks parade and polo grounds were just a camp of would-be amateur aviators.

Among thousands of aerial enthusiasts, the two Vancouver lovebirds agreed to rise 1,000 feet aloft and wed. According to *Polks 1911*, Henry lived at 512 W. Main Street and was a driver for Vancouver Soda Works. Because women lived with men or with their families, Nina's address is harder to pin down using Polks. Only two addresses would seem to fit, Ira Stanely at 200 W. 16th Street or Newell Stanely at 715 18th Street.

Henry and Nina imagined dreamily lifting off the ground as two individuals, then floating suspended between heaven and earth, exchanging vows, trading rings, kissing and descending bound as one in marriage. Likely their initial thought of a romantic vehicle was a balloon and not an airplane, for most planes of the day struggled to lift two people into the air. For the ceremony, their clergyman would need to be a wing walker. We do not know their thoughts, but they smacked of modernity, and the Claussen-Stanly marriage was on the forefront of aviation events, even aviation history. Or so they thought.

To the uninformed, a balloon might seem more sensible. In a balloon, the yet unwedded might squeeze a minister and a witness into the basket. Balloons have been sailing for more than a hundred years. There were several local flights.

April of 1890, the City of Vancouver's first balloon ascent took Professor William Lang skyward. He floated aloft from 13th Street reaching 500 or 600 feet. Local papers dubbed this modest ascension a success. The next year at the corner of 12th and Main Streets, Professor Vilas lifted of going beyond Lang's height and reaching 800 feet as about

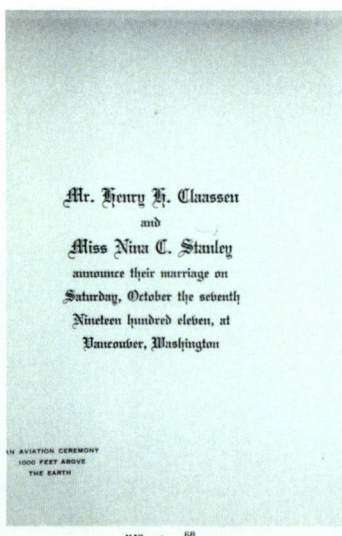

Mr. Henry H. Claussen
and
Miss Nina C. Stanley
announce their marriage on
Saturday, October the seventh
Nineteen hundred eleven, at
Vancouver, Washington

AN AVIATION CEREMONY
1000 FEET ABOVE
THE EARTH

MAY · 68

Claussen-Stanley Wedding invitation
(Source: Clark County Historical Museum cchm00423)

1500 Vancouverites watched. Vilas also made the first parachute jump in the county for when his balloon reached 800 feet, he bailed out with his parachute landing nearly atop a picket fence. (Nothing is said about how the balloon came down.)

A 1911 issue of *The Columbian* noted that Dick Miller launched his balloon on July 4th some years back. Miller, who evidently lacked both the professorial skills of a Lang and the foresight of a Vilas who dropped to earth under silk, descended not on dry land but in the wetness of the Columbia River, from which he had to be rescued. (Walker, 13)

Although no launched balloon had reached 1,000 feet in the local sky, a balloon wedding seemed more reasonable than an airplane. The soon-to-be newlyweds might at least squeeze a clergyman and a witness into the basket. How the bride might enter and exit the balloon basket gracefully wasn't publicized.

While anything that went aloft attracted a crowd, the public longed to see heavier-than-air flights. Two rivals, the Wright Brothers and Glenn Curtiss pulled together professional flying teams to assuage audiences' desire through exhibitions. Like Roman audiences viewing carnage from Coliseum seats, exhibition audiences quickly tired of viewing the same feats. Their attention wandered and kept they demanded more daring exploits. Pilots foolishly risked their lives and made money, even if many didn't live to spend their proceeds. (Walker, 19)

Flying was a high-risk feat at the time. Lincoln Beachey, who twice dirigibled over Vancouver, and Silas Christofferson, who flew off the Multnomah Hotel, both died in airplane crashes. The same year the betrothed couple sought an aerial conjugal, Harriet Quimby, a New York journalist, earned her pilot's license. She brought a sense of style to flying, wearing her trademark purple satin flying suit. She, too, died in an accident near Boston in 1912. However, each airplane accident or death never lessened the public's excitement for watching the bi-winged daredevils.

A Balloon near Esther Short Park in Vancouver (Source: CCHM cchm00477)

Was an aerial wedding valid? Before lawyers determined the wedding's legal status, seven more local couples signed up to take aerial nuptials.

Days before the October 7 wedding date, the eight brides wanted assurance that their nuptial knots would bind their partners as tightly as a wedding in a church. One bride appealed to a lawyer. When one Vancouver lawyer offered an opinion, other lawyers chimed in without reaching a consensus, creating confusion and anxiety about the weddings.

James Stapleton, Clark County attorney for four years, declared a wedding aloft illegal. To make it legal, the ceremony must be repeated on state soil. Stapleton said the license issued was for Washington State and nowhere else, including among the clouds. He asserted that if the pair were floating in the air, they would not be in the state. Attorney Fred Tempes conceded he needed to research that fine point. A good choice. In the early days of aviation, the concept of air space was still undefined. Perhaps the state attorney general should decide, another lawyer suggested.

Newspapers across the state, broke the news about the illegality of the airborne wedding. For example, the October 3 *Spokesman-Review* carried an article replace with more details about whether an aloft wedding was even legal, while suggesting the bride may have been having second thoughts herself:

The legality of the aviation wedding to take place in a balloon at the Clark County harvest show next Saturday has been questioned and several of the leading attorneys of Vancouver differ on the question.... The question of the legality of the ceremony was first brought up by Miss Stanley, who wanted to know that the knot would be tied as good and hard as it would be if the wedding took place in a church. When asked, the county attorney, Fred W. Tempes, said he would look up the point. It was a new one to him. James P. Stapleton, former county attorney for four years, said that the ceremony would be Illegal, and to make the marriage ceremony legal and binding it would have to be performed again on terra firma. He gave as his reason that the license was issued to be used in Washington and no other place, and if the couple were married in a balloon they, were not In Washington. It is likely that the matter will be taken up with the state attorney general at Olympia before the ceremony takes place. ("Question")

The threat of the state attorney general's involvement in establishing the legality of in-air marriages remained up in the air. Meanwhile, the Clark County Harvest Days officials saw the advertising benefit for the fair and were scrambling to find a balloon. A balloon wedding would certainly attract crowds. It seemed that it wasn't the law that would halt the aerial nuptials but the lack of a balloon. With no balloon to be found, they got creative. How might they pull off such a wedding without a balloon?

Emil F. Komm, a local twenty-year-old amateur aviator, was already scheduled as an attraction. He'd built a monoplane from bamboo weighing 120 pounds in his garage. The plane was powered by an engine originally. He called it the lightest he'd ever created, and removing the engine turned it into a glider. For several years before World War I broke out, Komm's name appeared in the local papers explaining his inventions.

In August 1911, the glider towed behind an automobile at the military field lifted off the ground using a car to pull it. Dragged behind a car Komm floated three feet off the ground in his engineless Santos-Dumont-Dleroit style airplane, which weighed a mere 120 pounds, the lightest airplane yet to be made. Its wing surface was 180 square feet. It never flew again. (Walker, 21) After the brief flight of his bamboo glider, Komm told the *Vancouver Columbian* reporter on the scene that he planned to fly it at the upcoming Clark County Harvest Fair. The youthful flier

Emil Komm's funeral record 1916 Source: *Washington State Death Records*

would use a 60-horsepower airplane engine and give free exhibitions every day at the fair in October. ("Monoplane")

At the County Harvest days, there were no exhibitions. Instead, the light-weight plane was used for a backdrop for a wedding. The airborne weddings planned for a balloon were grounded. Only one was performed with Komm's flightless plane used as a backdrop. (Walker, 21) First Presbyterian Church Rev. H. S. Templeton presided over the Claussen-Stanley wedding. Without leaving the earth, the pair exchanged nuptials with Komm's unusual screw-prop airplane behind them.

But the budding aviator-inventor wasn't done. In 1912, Komm sought to prove the efficiency of a small gasoline engine. The machine could fly with wings, or with them detached, roll along the roadway as a 13-foot-long car on three wheels, two under the engine and one in the rear. The driver sat in the vehicle's body which was constructed "like a coffin and offers practically no resistance to the air." The propeller is changed from the driver's seat. On the soft racetrack at the county fairgrounds, Komm did the trip in two minutes with the engine only open 25 percent yet reaching 30 miles an hour on the level ground. Circling the track, Komm said he felt his control slipping so he stopped the engine just as a control wire snapped, spilling him and pinning him in the car. Without wings the car weighed 200 pounds, but the wings add a little more. ("Modest")

For three months, "the young aeronaut of Vancouver," spent his nights and Sundays off working until midnight in a basement. The vehicle needed to be disassembled to remove it from the basement. This is the third airplane he built. ("Hydroplane")

In a 1913 attempt, as reported by the *Oregonian*, Komm had partnered with Bryan Fry to put his efforts into another "Airauto." The machine rolled down Eleventh Streets before Fry turned the engine wide open "flying along the pavement" at 50 miles an hour. An unfortunate dog ran out to chase the unique propellor-driven car only to be crushed under a wheel, bouncing the car two feet off the ground. Fry used similar designs to skim along the surface of Columbia River riding on pontoons. The inventors promised more trials, which appear to have been ignored. ("Airauto")

December 1912, Komm advertised his wedding plane for sale in Popular Mechanics. Whether it sold is unclear. Komm, however, joined the Army as a private and served at Kelly Field Aero Squadron 327. After his 1916 death, he was buried in the Tahoma Cemetery in Yakima, Washington. Although it's unlikely that Komm's plane ever flew under its own power, it did serve in an "aviation-like" wedding.

Martin Middlewood is the editor of Clark County History and writes a weekly column, "Images from the Attic," in The Columbian.

WORKS CITED

"Airauto Has Speed," *Oregonian*, December 17, 1913, p. 7.

"Hydroplane May Be Tried on the River Sunday," *The Columbian*, August 14, 1913, p. 1.

"Modest Inventor Furthers Aviation," *Oregonian*, June 22, 1912, p.4.

"Monoplane Leaves Ground with Auto Attached on Cable," *Vancouver Columbian*, Aug. 5, 1911.

"Monoplane Leaves Ground with Auto Attached on Cable," *The Columbian*, August 5, 1911, p. 1.

Polk's 1911.

"Question of Validity of Air Wedding," *The Spokesman-Review*, October 3, 1911, p. 16.

Walker, Jon. *A Century Airborne: Air Trails of Pearson Airpark*. Pioneer Printing, Vancouver, Washington, 1994.

LOOKING BACK

Single Mother Served as Teacher and Administrator

Oral history. Rujean "Jeanne" Mack considers her career

Interview and transcription, Steve Becker

Q: What was going on in your life that made you decide to become a teacher?

A: It was a result of a divorce and I had to find a way to make a living and provide for my children. It was 1967, I think and the options for work for women were limited. At least, in my view. I know there are many women who went on to do more than that, but it was true in my case. Teaching turned out to be the most efficient way to have an income.

Q: Did you have a college degree?

A: I wasn't even thinking about becoming a teacher. I was a music major at Clark College and did most of my classes at night. But when my youngest daughter, Karen entered kindergarten that allowed me to take a few daytime classes. So, I had reached, almost, the two years it would require me to get my degree in music and a minor in math. But the divorce happened before I finished. I went to my counselor to tell him I would be dropping out and he said "...that would

Jeanne Mack

be the stupidest mistake of your life." He said you talk to my instructors and make sure I get those 10 hours in and graduate. With that kind of encouragement, I proceeded to go to work and work with my instructors to do the work that needed to be done for my graduation. One of the classes was a pottery class because I needed the credit, and I went at night, and amazingly I found that it was very relaxing.

Q: You mentioned a moment ago that in 1967, there were few options for a woman in your situation. If you could have done anything professionally, what would you have done?

A: I am not sure. I wanted to go to college when I graduated from high school, and I loved math. Later in life, I realized with that math interest and some work that I had done at the phone company in the engineering department, the two went together very well, and I might have gone in that direction.

Q: How did you make the leap with a two-year associates degree to teaching?

A: I went to work for the phone company which I had worked for when I was in high school, and I got a call one day from my counselor. I wish I could remember his name; he was wonderful. He called me up and said "...How would you

Fruit Valley class photo 1973

like to teach?" I said that would be lovely, but I don't have my degree and he said he thought we could work something out. It was interesting that at that time, there was a big shortage of teachers, which currently happens to be the case. He said I want you to go to St. Joseph's Catholic Church, and they have a school, and I would like you to meet Sister Catherine Louise. I went, and we talked, and she said I think we can get you an emergency [teaching] certificate. It was kind of a back doorway to get into teaching.

Q: You did not have a college degree and presumably you did not have any training as a teacher or in managing a classroom. You just went into a classroom one day and started teaching? Was it that easy?

A: Well, amazingly, it was. One of the things that was in my favor was that because it was a Catholic school, all the students were trained to be extremely polite and responsive, so I didn't have to be a disciplinarian. I simply had to teach what the curriculum said I needed to teach. The biggest challenge was in math where they had introduced what they called the "new math" the year before. The 8th graders I taught were learning what I had learned in high school, and high school had been a long way back. So, I spent a lot of time figuring that out. But because the kids were responsive, it was an easy job. I read what their lesson was and researched what I needed to research, and taught the lesson

Q: What do you remember about your first classroom?

A: I can see that first classroom as clear as day. It had the religious statuary, and right in front of me was Mike Wilson, who was a boy from Scotland; black hair and blue eyes. He was very quiet and just looked at me all the time I was teaching. I don't remember all the other kids except for a few; they were wonderful students. I also taught them music which is what I had been more focused on than anything else, and that was fun. I taught them about the music I loved, and I asked them about the music they loved, and we both played, and that was probably a brilliant idea because they responded very well to the music I loved if I listened to the music they loved.

Q: What music did you play for them?

A: I don't recall the specific recordings I shared with them, but I did involve them in reductions of opera, and opera was not something I was terribly fond of; I was more into instrumental music. But these reductions caught my eye, and we did a production of *The Marriage of Figaro* by Rossini, and we did *The Man from The Moon* by Hayden, and we did the *HMS Pinafore*. In the three years, we were there, we did three musical productions, and I think probably those captured their interest as much as anything I could teach them. They were completely involved either on stage or backstage or making the programs, or being involved in building the sets. It was a very successful way to have them engage in music.

Q: Do you remember what music they wanted you to listen to?

A: I don't. But it was the same music that my kids were listening to; it was the music of the day. I should recall some of those, but they don't come to mind. My mind is so filled with classical music.

Q: You are a divorced woman with no teaching certificate teaching in a Catholic school. How were you received in that community?

A: At first, I thought very well. They also provided a way for me to finish my college degree by paying for it ahead. I couldn't afford the tuition, they would pay it, then deduct a portion of it from my monthly check, so they provided a way for me to get my degree.

Q: You were working and going to school at the same time?

Sister Catherine Louise, principal of St. Joseph's School in the late 1960's, helped launch Jeanne Mack's career as an educator. (Photo credit: St. Joseph's School)

A: I was working going to school, and I had four children at home, and they learned to be my support system; they cooked dinner, picked up the house, and helped with my studying and listened to me play the piano a lot. We were a team, and on Saturday night, we had a good time, whether it was popcorn or television programs we loved to watch together. It was probably one of the most satisfying times of my life and the most intense in the sense that I had so many responsibilities: I had to teach a class and go to school and be with my family and make it work.

Q: *You were at St Joseph's for three years. What happened after that?*

A: After that, I received the news that I did not have a teaching certificate even though I had been teaching for three years. I hadn't gone through the system and had supervised teaching experience. I did not qualify to teach in a public school, and that was a big blow. That summer was probably the worst summer of my life. I smoked cigarettes and drank

St. Joseph's School opened ion September 8, 1954, with 302 students in grades 1-8.
(Photo credit: the author)

The current Fruit Valley Elementary School opened as a community learning center in 2002. (photo credit: the author)

coffee, and made appointments to see if I could get a job. I went everywhere. I remember going to a bank, to stores, and nothing seemed to work. And one day, I had an idea; I said you know, I need to be teaching. How am I going to make that work? I had gone to the Vancouver School District, and the person who I will never forget said you'll never teach here. It wasn't a very kind thing to say and very discouraging.

Q: Why did they say that? Did they have an explanation?

A: Simply that I didn't have supervised student teaching, and I explained to them that I taught for three years, and my supervisor was Sister Catherine Louise, and she was always satisfied with my work, but I had to have the piece of paper that said I was qualified to teach, and I didn't have it. So I had the idea one day that if the Vancouver School District would not let me in, I wonder if the Portland School District would be interested in me. They were right across the river, so I went to the central office, and I talked to a woman about my situation, and she looked at me. She said, you know, I have an idea, and she left and came back with a piece of paper and said there is a federal program to help people get their degrees, and the two criteria were you needed to be black and poor, and I only met the poverty criterion. She said let me work on this; the deadline is almost here. I'll see if I can get you in, and she did. I finished my degree. I was supervised, I took classes that added to my college degree and after one year was ready to go back into the Vancouver system. I could have gotten a job in Portland, but I wanted to work in Vancouver. I went to the Vancouver School District and showed them my paperwork, and a different person said you are hired. There was still a teacher shortage, and they were anxious to have me.

Q: Where did you go to work in the Vancouver Schools?

A: I interviewed at two schools: One was Franklin and one was Fruit Valley. Franklin was in a nice neighborhood and Fruit Valley was having a difficult time with poverty and drugs and all kinds of things. I interviewed at both places, and the response from Franklin was we are really looking for a man, and I am sure you could not say that today. But later, the Franklin principal later called me and said, you know, I'd like to hire you. But because of the previous conversation I thought no way. You want a man? They wanted a man at Fruit Valley too. But the principal at Fruit Valley, Millie Collins, was the first female principal in the Vancouver School District, and she talked with me and said I think you can do this; I think this would be a good match, and I was hired in about 1971 at Fruit Valley.

Q: What was Fruit Valley like? How did it compare to St. Joseph's School?

A: There were some marvelous kids. But the respect for the teacher was lacking by many, especially the boys. I'm sure that 6th-grade class, I'm sure every principal in the district wanted a man, not a woman, in a 6th-grade class because they seemed to have more control over the boys. They were very unruly, and the biggest thing was I had 6th graders who could not read, and I had never taken a class in teaching kids how to read. That was a real shock. How do I help these kids learn how to read?

Q: How did you do that?

A: We had several strategies, and one of them was we had kids teaching kids how to read. We recorded our reading, and some of our kids had dyslexia or other eye issues, and they could not read. But they could listen to the story, and one girl in particular would read out loud word for word, but she would miss a couple of words, so I knew she was memorizing the story. That was very challenging, but I also had that class do a reduction of the opera *Aida*. A young man in my class who could not read had low self-esteem and was kind of a bully turned out to be a great actor. He learned every line, he was the star of the show, and the teachers were just shocked because he had been labeled as a non-reader, as a disruptive child. So sometimes, if you find something a child can excel in, it changes a lot for them.

Q: Were these strategies that were suggested to you, or were they things you improvised along the way?

A: The operettas were a key to a lot of the teaching I did. I don't know that anybody I knew had done those, and I don't remember them being done in school. But music was the answer to having a relationship with kids in which they could be successful, and because of that, they tried harder at everything they did. It even improved their ability to behave in class. I think we learned to respect each other. Not that there weren't times when kids weren't way out of control. Do you want to hear the story about the one that was expelled?

Go right ahead.

I can see him. He would stand up on desks and make the lights swing, and the whole class just egged him on. He would end up being sent home and would be out for three days, and then we would go through it again. Finally, it came to the point where the parents thought it was my fault. I probably blamed them; I didn't say that to them. This child was really out of control. So, after he had been sent home several times, the principal and I agreed there needed to be further disciplinary action. He became the first student in a Vancouver School District elementary school to be expelled from school. That doesn't feel good. But the other kids couldn't learn with him there.

Q: *Do you know whatever happened to him?*

A: The whole family had difficult situations to deal with, and I am almost certain he did not graduate from high school.

Q: *Did your experience at this time, early in your career at Fruit Valley, influence how you approached issues around discipline later in your career?*

A: Absolutely. If I could have been the counselor at Fruit Valley, I think I could have worked with the family of the student who had been expelled. But this was so unusual. Fifty years ago, kids weren't as disruptive back then. That sounds terrible. I don't think kids had as many issues. Poverty and drugs were the big issue at Fruit Valley. What I knew was you had to find a way to reach a child, and I think I learned that when I provided other things for kids to do, other than just sticking their noses in a book and giving them a test. When you get to know the kids, when you are doing something like production, you get to learn something about them; you get to know them. They grow as young people, and you get to know what their gifts are. The need for discipline is lessened, but you

Fruit Valley became part of Vancouver Public Schools in 1915 when the Fruit Valley School District consolidated with Vancouver Public Schools. (photo credit: the author)

will still have discipline problems. I learned to engage the child, listen to the child and discipline is the last thing you want to do. You want to find a solution in a way that they can be successful.

Q: What was the typical approach to discipline in those days?

A: Mostly, they were sent home, and, in some schools, they just gave them a whack.

Q: Corporal punishment?

A: Yes. That wasn't true at the school where I was, but I had heard it was still being done in other schools. I tried to motivate positive behaviors. I collected teddy bears. These wonderful women brought them in wicker baskets, like laundry baskets and here were all these teddy bears. If the kids were good, they could go to the principal's office to pick out a teddy bear. Every month we had a birthday party for the kids who had a birthday that month and fed them bologna sandwiches and bananas and potato chips, and they could pick out a teddy bear. It was something to see these 6th-grade boys come into my office and pick out a teddy bear. One of the 6th graders said I'm taking this home to my brother, and he probably was. But a lot of them took a teddy bear and enjoyed them, I'm sure.

Q: How long were you a classroom teacher?

A: I was a classroom teacher for three years. I then taught half-time and then worked on curriculum half-time, and you know, it escapes me for how many years I did that. It may have been two or three.

Q: How long did you work on the curriculum?

A: It became a focus. The superintendent called me one day and said how would you like to be a principal, the principal of Fruit Valley? With that I moved from a classroom/curriculum person to a principal and because it was a small school, I still was required to do curriculum and eventually, I was also given the Challenge Program, so I supervised a program for gifted kids and was principal in a school with kids who lived in poverty.

Q: Why do you think the superintendent approached you about being principal at Fruit Valley?

A: You know, I have always wondered about that. I really don't know how my name would come up except that I had done some presentations in curriculum, and I was using some equipment that was not used by everyone, early computer times. It was pretty basic. But he was impressed by that, I'm sure.

Q: *You mentioned that a lot of the kids at Fruit Valley were very poor. Did you have to put new systems in place to address their poverty and their needs?*

A: When I was principal, I asked the superintendent to come down and take a tour of the area. One of the places we toured was the (neighborhood) mobile home park. If you drive through the trailer park where many kids lived, there was garbage all over the place. It was the dirtiest, most unhealthy environment. I am not sure how significant that mobile home park was, but there were a lot of trailers in there, and he was shocked, he was shocked, and he talked to one of the state legislators and said, you know, you need to come down and see what this is like. He had a bus load of influential people come in. His purpose was trying to find resources that could support and help these people overcome their way of life. He was successful in doing that. I think he was impressed that I even asked him to come down and I was further impressed because he came down and saw to it that things were done differently.

Q: *Which superintendent was this?*

A: Jim Parsley.

Q: *What changed at Fruit Valley after that visit?*

A: When I was principal at Fruit Valley I made sure the kids who were good got to come in to see me. The kids who were having problems had to sit in the outer office with something to keep their hands busy like clay or a puzzle or something until I was free and had time to talk with them. And we would try to problem solve together: What they did wrong, what they could do about it and how they were feeling. Usually how they were feeling came first because if they were angry or upset you have to find out why and then you can begin problem solving.

Q: *Is it true that when you were a student, was brought to you by a teacher who demanded you "paddle" or spank the student?*

A: Actually, that was when I was being trained to be a principal, and my mentor told me my job that day was to spank this child because he had been disruptive. I think it was actually because he didn't get his work done. Anyway, I refused. I said I could not spank children.

Q: *Why is that?*

A: Well, I think that kind of punishment is cruel. You aren't solving the problem; you are making the problem worse.

Q: There was an episode at Fruit Valley when you were visited by a Secret Service Agent. Do you remember that?

A: Oh, my goodness. I haven't thought about that in a long time. It was Christmas break, and I was there, and he walked into the school and said you know, we are checking out this house across the street, and he said can we set up here? So they went into the library, and they watched the house across the street and eventually they moved in and arrested a group of counterfeiters; they got their man.

Q: *How long were you a principal?*

A: Three years at Fruit Valley, then I moved on to three years at Washington Elementary School.

Q: *Is it true that you helped found the Family Connections Resource Centers (FCRC) program in Vancouver Schools?*

A: That came about from the wonderful planning sessions that the district put on when they were going to build a new Fruit Valley School. As part of that process, you dream about what would be the ideal thing for that school. And a lot of our dreams that we suggested were a little grandiose and over the top.

At our table, when it finally came down to it, we suggested they have a separate room for families to come and have some training and have computers available and have somebody available to help them and we said we wanted early childhood education. As it turned out, that school was built, my goodness what year was that? I should recall that. I was still at Fruit Valley when that school was built, so I remember leaving the school knowing they wouldn't be going back to the old building. Anyway, the result was that those ideas stuck. They had an early childhood program, and they had a room that was called the family resource center.

Q: *What kind of help could families get in a family resource center?*

A: We were focused on helping parents learn. But it became a place where their needs were shared, problem-solving began, and we got resources to families. That is kind of when one of my jobs came into focus when I was the director of the Vancouver Schools Foundation. Actually, before that. When I was at Fruit Valley as principal, these two wonderful ladies, Shirley Galloway and Peggy Lansverk were focused on helping kids in need, and they had a shoe box. They collected money, I do not know how, but they had a shoe box with money in it, and they took it to Jim Parsley and said we want to help kids in need. So, I could request a pair of shoes if a child needs them, and they provided the money. Eventually, they made it possible for me to have a checkbox with one hundred dollars in it, and I could spend it on whatever the kids' needs were. So that was the beginning of check books in the schools, and it grew to five schools and now every principal has the opportunity because at this point, district wide, every school has an FCRC coordinator who will see to it that the needs of the kids are met either through the foundation or contributions.

Q: *You eventually transitioned into administration. How did that come about?*

A: I think it's because I had been doing the work in curriculum and I'm sure that Jim Parsley again said we can use you in administration. I worked on a math program that was funded through a federal program and we took it back to

Washington DC and it was approved for distribution. I spent some time traveling and sharing what became the HOSTS Math program. I wrote a lot of the curriculum, Jim Parsley said I wrote all of it, but I had the help of Bill Hogan who was a secondary teacher. I had taught math in elementary schools and had learned a lot about how kids needed to learn. Many of our books had samples of problems that you had to solve, and the next step was to make it clear how to solve the problem. Many of the kids needed to go back to counting things and seeing the process visually. In other words, if you have 3 + 2 three blocks and two blocks help them see the relationship. But if it just says 3 + 2 it's a mystery to some kids.

Q: You had different roles in the administration of the Vancouver School District. What were some of them?

A: I was the director of the Challenge Program for high achieving kids getting scores in the 95th percentile. They went to different schools and had different teachers and I understand

Rujean on bassMusic remains a big part of Jeanne Mack's life, June 2023. (photo credit: the author)

it lasted until just this last year when it was dissolved. It wouldn't have been dissolved if Jim Parsley was there. I worked in curriculum. Then became the first executive director of the Vancouver Schools Foundation and the foundation grew because the math program I helped develop was sold for $50,000 and Jim Parsley sent that money to the foundation.

Q: It is ironic to you that you started working in a school with impoverished kids and you learned how to support their needs and then ended up running the foundation to benefit all students?

A: Oh yes. But boy, was that a job where I was dedicated and believed in it. I was so glad to see those checkbooks go from five schools to all the schools and for the programs we believed in to go to all the schools where the support for families and children is a priority. That was very rewarding.

Q: Looking back on your career, how did your experiences shape you as a person?

A: It was rewarding in a number of ways. The things that I believed in I was able to implement and make a difference in children's lives. It was very rewarding, it really was.

Q: What is it like to hear from your former students.

A: I hear from the students at St. Joe's. I feel like I'm still friends with my first class. I don't hear from the kids at Fruit Valley, but I did run into one who was an Uber driver. She was driving me past Fruit Valley School toward downtown Vancouver and she said oh yes, I went to Fruit Valley. I said you did? I said I was the principal at Fruit Valley, too. She said she never got into trouble....except once. She and a group of friends skipped class in the 6th grade.

I remembered that was the day half the 6th grade class went to a house and to have a party. It was so obvious. I knew right off that with half the class absent, they weren't all sick. So, I checked around and the rumor was they had drugs so I called the police and the police went to the house and brought all the kids in. There weren't any drugs, but we had to keep our kids safe. My Uber driver was one of those kids. She gave me a big hug when she dropped me off.

Q: If you had to do it all over again when you have been a teacher again?

A: It was very rewarding. But who knows if I had other options what I would have done. I have no idea. What I do know is that I enjoyed teaching very much. It was fun to find things that would interest kids and help young people be all they could be.

Transcribed from an interview conducted December 3, 2022 and has been edited for length and clarity. The interviewer, Steve Becker, is Rujean Mack's son.

Silver Star Indigenous Native Pits

Gene Ritter

The Silver Star Indigenous Pits are among the more popular hiking destinations for local residents but there are others on Archer and Wind Mountains in the Columbia Gorge. More pits have been found by hunters as far away as Sublette Mountain in Wyoming.

Archaeologists can only guess as to how the pits may have fit into ancient culture. One theory is that young Indigenous Americans seeking a spiritual vision would sit isolated in the pits for days. Another idea is that the pits were used as hunting blinds for hunting mountain sheep and goats fleeing cougars or wolves down the slopes. One thing is for sure, a lot of time and effort went into constructing them.

Silver Star Mountain is a great place for hiking and seeing the Indigenous Native Pits is well worth the modest hike. Keep in mind a Discover Pass is required.

Google Earth shows cairns in upper right quadrant.

Close-up of Silver Star Indigenous cairn. Photo by author.

The best access to the pits is from Grouse Vista trailhead on the 1200 Road. The first part of the hike is rather steep on Pyramid Rock trail No. 180F. The ancient native pits trail in No. 180E. Trail numbers can be confusing in the area because U. S. Forest Service trail numbers do not coincide with the Washington Department of Natural Resources numbers.

If you know where to look, the pits show up well on Google Earth.

Looking over an a Silver Star cairn. Photo by author.

Gene Ritter's grandparents arrived in Clark County in 1905. A retired real estate broker, he is interested in histories of the county's donation land claims and historic places around the county, Gene has often contributed to Clark County History.

Wily woman scams railroads

Called "Accident Queen" or "Queen of the Fakirs" by the press

Martin Middlewood

At the Clark County Courthouse in 1910, Judge A.L. Miller's opening remarks in a fraud trial ran a wearisome three hours. In legalese, he struggled to explain and unwind the knotted skein of facts involving a series of fraudulent accident payouts perpetuated by the infamous Maud Johnson before trying her for fraud in his Vancouver courtroom. He explained how Johnson faked injuries while traveling between Vancouver and Yacolt on the railroad. For the alleged injury, she received $1,250 from D. C. Davis, a railroad claims agent. While this was but one of her many criminal acts, it was the one that brought her to the Clark County jail and then the courthouse. Her trial would expose many of her other scams.

Headlined as the "Accident Queen" and the "Queen of Fakirs" [sic] by the press, Maud Johnson's local case involved a complex web of interrelated crimes she'd committed over several years and in several states under false names, including Nellie Martin, Mrs. M. L Harlson, Maude Thomas, Mrs. Grace Peyton, Miss Maud Myrtle Johnson, Edith Strong, and Rose Carey. Judge Miller wanted the defendant and her lawyer to know that after years of getting paid for accident hoaxes, the law was onto her.

Sometimes Maud of many names posed as a wealthy, grieving widow whose husband had recently passed. Frequently, she portrayed a single, vulnerable woman. At other times, she posed as a mother, using children as props to gain the sympathy of railroad agents—and extort more rapid and profitable settlements. Over several years cloaked in these identities, she defrauded nearly every railroad west of the

Mississippi, wresting payments for multiple bogus injuries. Faking an injury, she'd loudly chastise her victim, knowingly setting her scene for any adverse publicity that might sully any transportation company's reputation.

Johnson, born on an Albany, Oregon farm as Maud Myrtle Wagnon, started her criminal life early. After her mother died, her father put her in a convent. As a fourteen-year-old, she sued a man for seduction, claiming he had promised to marry her. She received payment for this first extortion, which later became her preferred technique. She ran away from the convent at 16, drifting into vaudeville. Police in the larger Oregon cities knew her as a petty criminal. (Finn)

Judge Miller explained Johnson claimed injuries in Seattle, Oakland and cities across the west to a courtroom filled with Vancouver's prominent men and women and curious students interested in seeing this one-woman crime wave. Maud Johnson was a mediocre-looking woman of average weight and height, with a hooked nose set on her narrow asymmetric face and extending beyond her slightly receding chin. The courtroom audience probably wondered how such a moderately attractive woman duped railroad personnel. Maybe they thought her sad-looking hazel eyes made her look needy. Or perhaps, her rowdy demeanor intimidated them. Or maybe she called on a lawsuit if she met resistance. Or was she just a compulsive liar? We will never know.

Johnson's defense attorney pleaded that his client was a poor woman unable to defend herself

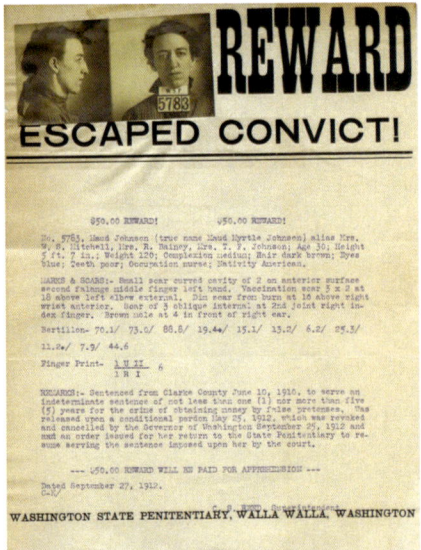

Maud Johnson Wanted Poster
(Source: Washington State Archives)

against 15 to 30 charges coming at her from nearly as many states and railroads. But her lawyer posited that the injury she received on the Yacolt line was real since its agent voluntarily paid her. What went unsaid was that Johnson could repeat her fraud because the railroads didn't relish either lawsuits or bad publicity. Both were bad for business.

The afternoon of the Yacolt incident, Johnson was carrying a suitcase in one arm and a child in the other. The conductor helped her board the train, and she asked to be seated by the door. She told him to place her valise nearby where she could easily access it (or perhaps even trip over it).

The train left the old depot near the Vancouver ferry landing, pulling out at about 4:30 p.m. It stopped briefly in Barberton, where the train slowed and halted. The stop wasn't jarring, but Johnson became raucous, contended she was hurt, and spat out blood. Alarmed, the conductor made her a cot, trying to comfort her and straightening her ankle, which, she said, she'd placed on the footrest and wrenched it during the stop. She also complained of an injured wrist.

As she swooned and fainted, someone offered her a glass of water as the train clattered onto Yacolt. Mistakenly, Johnson accepted it in the hand she'd declared damaged. When an onlooker pointed out she was using her hurt hand, the glass slid from her grasp, spilling on the floor.

At Yacolt, passengers carried Maud to Dr. McMordo's infirmary on a stretcher, where she resisted every examination attempt because she now declared she also had heart disease, making any review too painful for her to bear. Johnson compounded her troubled narrative by claiming she had never been in an accident.

Maud's story soon extended from barely credible to unbelievable, and she changed her name in the process. She told investigator D. C. Davis she was Hazel Peterson, a widow who traveled to Yacolt to examine a tract of timberland her dead husband owned. This and property in Calgary now were the property of the child she carried on the train. (The child seems to have curiously vanished after Johnson's arrival in Yacolt.) She demanded that officials return her to Yacolt. Days after the alleged accident, she added eye problems to the list of her complaints but never explained the cause.

Claims agent Davis settled with her shortly after. Mid-week, as Johnson feigned complete helplessness, men carried her to the train for her return to Vancouver. There, they brought her limp body into a hotel room. Two nurses were assigned to travel with her to Calgary.

Conveniently Johnson's injuries prevented her from seeing the Yacolt timberland once owned by her dead husband, yet she intended to see his property in Canada despite her frailty. Although she claimed never to have been in an accident prior, officials soon discovered that she'd been in a dozen or more. When her supposed brother-in-law came to retrieve her, he claimed never to have seen her.

Somehow, as her nurses watched, Johnson arranged for someone to pick her up and skedaddled to Oregon City. When her so-called husband showed up, he hightailed it away the following day. But that wasn't quite a clean getaway. A claim agent named Day recognized them aboard the Southern Pacific headed to California. Johnson had cheated him in the past. Agent Day told the conductor to keep an eye on the two grifters. Another railroad detective followed them to Los Angles.

In his lengthy preamble to the trial and over the defense's objection, Judge Miller noted that Johnson, as far back as July 1907, had defrauded the Southern Pacific in Los Angeles. Then in September, she repeated her crime in Kansas City while stepping off a streetcar and falling over her suitcase, a prop Johnson used in several of her crimes. For that accident, she received $35. Before the month was out, Johnson had another accident in Rogers, Arkansas claiming to be Rose Carey before lapsing into speechlessness. In Colorado Springs, she defrauded

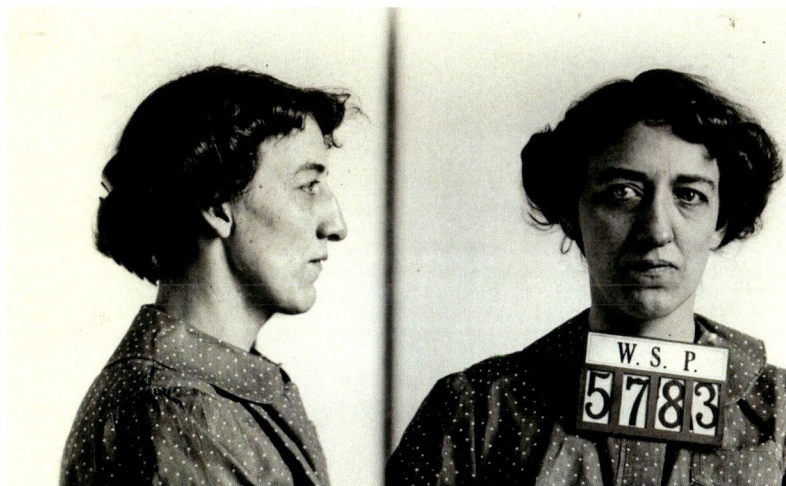

Maud Johnson mug shot.   *(Source: Washington State Archives)*

the Pullman Company for $500. Then Johnson, posing as Mrs. Preston, concocted yet an accident in Gold Hill, Oregon.

Traveling to Harrington, Kansas, in December 1908 and assuming the role of an author named Myrtle Johnson, she fell off a motorcar. In January 1909, she journeyed to Eureka Springs, Arkansas, as Maud Myrtle Johnson, where she assumed the railroad would pay her again, but this time it rejected her shady claim.

Posing as Nellie Martin, a wealthy widow, Johnson hit Pullman, Washington and Genesee, Idaho, gaining a $350 payoff during September. The following month, she was a wealthy widow and Eastern Star member, Mrs. M. L Harlson, and while asserting she was chasing down a woman who had stolen her furs, faked another injury. When approached by an Eastern Star member, Maud failed to recognize the secret signs. Again, she fled.

Also in October, Johnson became Mrs. Maude Thomas in Sterling, Nebraska. She told the claims agent that she'd lost her purse and cash, and the railroad gave her $400. That same month, posing as Mrs. Grace Peyton, Johnson claimed the railroad almost killed her. To hush any scandal, the railroad paid her $250. She fled town immediately.

The many-aliased woman headed west, stopping in Springfield, Missouri, where she faked another accident as Miss Edith Strong. Her claim of a disjointed ankle was fouled when conductor Lemon pulled on her leg and said she didn't whimper. During Maud Johnson's Vancouver trial, Lemon appeared as a star witness recounting how she told him of her widowhood and heading to Yacolt to care for some timber nearby.

The state's witness, Dr. McMordo of Yacolt, explained he didn't want to impose an embarrassing examination when Johnson resisted all his attempts to evaluate her, refusing even a breast exam to check her heart rate. She squirmed as if intense pain saying her father had died while under an anesthetic. Under oath, the doctor stated that while he checked her eyes, he also felt her ankle and found no damage, and added that Maud's expectorant from the train wasn't blood but another substance.

Johnson's pratfalls proved lucrative enough to antagonize the railroads. To fight back, railroad investigators formed the Pacific Claims Agents Association to sort through all claims and flag any fraudulent ones. Then they went after Johnson. The organization alerted police across the west of Johnson and her crimes. (Finn) In August 1909, the new claims organization paid off. The Oakland police arrested Mrs. Maud Myrtle Johnson for a bogus claim against the Seattle Electrical Company and her Yacolt caper.

During the legal-jargon-ladened three-hour-long string of crimes Judge Miller unraveled in the courtroom, he demonstrated to the defendant that her reign of orchestrated accidents for sympathy and profit had ended. When the judge exposed the magnitude of Johnson swindling 19 railroad companies, Lady Justice's scales tilted toward guilty. The jury declared Johnson so, and the judge sentenced her to five years at Walla Walla prison.

The "Accident Queen" and the "Queen of the Fakirs" would go behind bars. But she wasn't inside Walla Walla prison for long. After serving two years, whether through charisma or behind-the-scenes effort, Johnson finagled a 1913 conditional pardon from Washington State Governor Marion Hay. True to form, she fled, breaking her parole. Maud Johnson likely turned to petty crimes to survive, such as forging checks, shoplifting or solicitation, so she'd not be discovered, leaving the big paychecks for pratfalls behind.

Martin Middlewood is the editor of Clark County History and writes the weekly column "Images from the Attic" for The Columbian, where a shorter version of this article appeared.

Works Cited

Finn J.D. John, "Albany woman should be in Swindlers Hall of Fame," May 29, 2016, https://offbeatoregon.com/1605e.maud-johnson-queen-o-fakirs-393.html

"Queen of the Fakirs," *The Columbian*, August 8, 1908, p. 3.

"Thread Of Strange Story is Traced," *The Columbian*, April 26, 1910, pp. 1, 3.

Washington State Archives (photo) Corrections Department, Washington State Penitentiary, Commitment Registers and Mug Shots, 1887-1946 – Maud – Johnson – Ar129-5-8-Ph005783, https://digitalarchives.wa.gov/News/View/126

Washington State Archives, Treasures of the Archives: Wanted: Maud Johnson: "Queen of Fakirs," https://digitalarchives.wa.gov/News/View/126

FROM THE STAFF

Caring for your museum's collection

Liza Schade, collections manager

As a passionate Pacific Northwest historian, working with the Clark County Historical Museum is a professional honor. Having the chance to "learn something new every day" is not just a cliché when caring for our museum's collections! Preserving and studying old objects provides a tangible connection to countless generations that came before us. We honor our ancestors and keep their memory alive by learning more about the items they once touched, used and left behind. Every artifact has historical context behind it: an 1849 leatherbound quartermaster's journal from the old Columbia Barracks (now Vancouver Barracks), Kaiser Shipyard photos taken by staff photographer Louis Lee, a 1952 Vancouver High School letters sweater, a vintage postcard collection of Vancouver street scenes, and the list goes on.

Our team strives to increase public access to collections and archival information. We hope to make guests and researchers feel the awe we do about all the artifacts and records preserved here. This year, the museum has a new exhibit called "Homegrown Historians," which showcases many rarities from our collection, such as a toolbox used at Kaiser Shipyards, a 1920s lime green wool swimsuit, and carved chunks of the famous Witness Tree. It features oral history interviews conducted by seventh-grade students from Our Lady of Lourdes School. The text panels contain information from local historian Carl Landerholm's four-volume history, "Cayuse to Cadillac."

Providing efficient access to museum materials is also a major priority. In the spring of 2023, the CCHM Collections Committee approved plans for updated archive and reference library organizational systems. We want to digitize more documents, maps, and photographs to store in the online repository shared with Washington State University Library.

The actual position of collections manager at CCHM includes a variety of duties. Caring for physical objects and maintaining paper records comes first. Thanks to newly approved plans, staff will begin reorganizing the archival and library collections, designate new location codes, and scan and catalog individual records. When researchers submit requests for information, our staff and volunteers can find and sort through records faster to provide an answer. We also want to keep consistently uploading photos and archival collections to make them accessible for public and academic study.

Collections managers also work with donors to take in and evaluate private collections, gathering information and submitting requests monthly to a collections committee. The group comprises several regional professionals from education, archaeology and collections who vote on each donation. We curate internal and external exhibits, from the largest gallery space to the smallest popup display. That is a fun part of the job because it is an opportunity to work with stakeholders and build educational, creative, aesthetically pleasing displays.

Collaboration with diverse community groups like Music Fusion and NAACP, training in artifact care and research, conducting oral history interviews, and consistently studying Pacific Northwest history is also an important responsibility. Nothing is better than paying forward our knowledge and skills to volunteers and interns, who are always needed to help with essential tasks like cataloging, exhibit planning, photo scanning and metadata, research and creating digital assets (such as videos and social media posts). Personally, no matter how fun-filled or tedious the task is, each day provides an opportunity to understand more about Pacific NW history and pay respect to all those who have cared about saving it. Hopefully, future historians will do the same for our generation decades from now.

Liza was raised in Portland and has worked in county collections since 2010. She earned a Master's in Public History from Portland State in 2021. Graduate thesis work focused on collections management, reinterpretation and public access to historic house museums. She loves caring for the CCHM collection, curating displays and working with community members.

BOOKMARKS

Fire in the Heartland, Timothy Egan

History may not repeat itself, but it does provide us with lessons learned. If you are someone who looks to history to understand what's happening today, then read about the rise and fall of the Ku Klux Klan in Indiana in Pulitzer Prize winner Tim Egan's book *Fire in the Heartland*.
In doing so you'll see parallels between the ascent and fall of David C. Stephenson, the Grand Dragon of the Indiana Klan, with our 45th president's troubles.

David C. Stephenson rolled into Indiana and ascended ruthlessly to power within the Klan and made that state the leader in KKK membership. He admired Mussolini and his actions. Stephenson took part of the proceeds of every membership, every robe and hood sold, as well as any literature.

A sadistic, treacherous schemer, he was a spiteful and hateful womanizer while wielding the power of the grand wizard of the Ku Klux Klan. He openly declared that he was above the law, in fact that he was the law. Egan's tale exposes the extremism and angry white supremacy of the 1920s, which reached millions of people at the time. Today the white supremacy attitude still stains our country.

The Indiana Grand Wizard fell because of his sin of pride. Stephenson pursued a 28-year-old single woman Madge Oberholtzer, living with her parents. Although she was often at parties at his mansion, she spurned his advances while

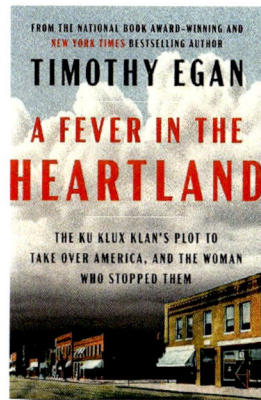

thinking Stephenson could stop the loss of her state job, yet she never trusted him enough to get married despite Stephenson's constant requests. Instead, she was kidnapped and drugged.

As she was dying, Oberholtzer recounted her ordeal, the transcript was presented in court supported by a doctor's similar testimony. The doctor claimed sepsis caused by Stephenson's deep bites to Oberholtzer's face, breasts, tongue, and other areas contributed as much to her demise as the poison she consumed and that she could have been saved had prompt action been taken.

But Stephenson wasn't worried about the charges. He ruled Indiana with a private army 30,000 fueled by graft and kickbacks, even the governor and many other officials were under his control. He felt confident he would be exonerated when he was taken to trial.

But he wasn't. He went to jail.

Roger Stark, *They Called Him Marvin*, Silver Star Publishing, Washougal, WA, 2021.

Roger Stark is a frequent contributor to *Clark County History* and has finished a nonfiction book about a recently married couple drawn into the depths of the Second World War and its effects on them and their families. The book is part epistolary because the author uses the letters passing between Dean and Connie Sherman.

One Sunday, Dean Sherman went to church in Salt Lake City with a new friend. From that point forward, he embarked unwittingly on a spectacular, valiant journey—falling in love with Connie, completing demanding training to become a B29 pilot, giving birth to a son, and joining the China, Burma, and India theater of World War II.

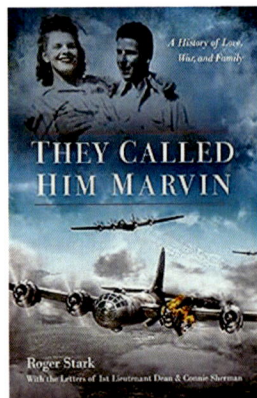

Every one of his missions presented difficulties, including minus fifty-degree weather in Mukden, Japanese firing at them, and a near collision with another B29 while flying sightlessly through clouds. He witnessed friends die because of a plane's mechanical failures and, like them, feared running out of fuel on long missions and engine fire, every pilot's greatest fear.

Dean wrote letters to Connie, narrating his story, not knowing that a Japanese swordsman would cut short his life just four and a half years later. He and his crew were shot down over Nagoya, Japan, as part of Mission 174. Captured, the Japanese transferred them to the Mariana Islands, imprisoned them, and declared them war criminals. None of the prisoners were allowed to correspond, even with families.

Connie's letters describe her life as a new mother while her husband was listed as missing in action. Designated a war criminal, Dean was imprisoned in Japan, while Connie bore the agony of not knowing why her husband's letters had stopped.

The book is a personal tale that draws the reader into the close relationship between the husband and wife rather than focusing on the conflict of war. Readers who enjoy how individuals are swept up in historical events, military history, or the impact of war on wives and families left alone, not knowing where their loved ones are, should consider Stark's book.

By his admission, Start says he's a reluctant writer. But he saw this story as sacred, affecting ordinary people in extraordinary circumstances. Stark is a former addiction counselor and has previously written two books on addiction recovery.

IN MEMORIAM

Franklin "Frank" William Emerick

1936-2022

Frank Emerick lived most of his life in North Clark County, preserving the history of that area. (Source: Emerick family)

Frank Emerick's hands dribbled basketballs around the LaCenter High gym as a teenage basketball player. When he courted his future wife, Roberta Ferguson, they carried roses to her. Eventually, they were married for 66 years. Roberta's parents owned the LaCenter Roller Rink, and to continue courting her, he learned to roller skate. Frank didn't speak about love often. Instead, his hands demonstrated his love when he held his children, grandchildren, nieces and nephews and when he restored North County history with his preservation of pioneer buildings.

After graduating high school, Frank attended Clark College and studied welding. He worked as a logger, an Air Force weather observer on Guam, an engineer for the forest service and as a mail carrier for International Paper. Released from the Air Force, Frank returned home to live in his grandparent's cabin and added additions twice for his family.

His energetic hands continued restoring things, antique cars, the Tum Tum cabin on Chelatchie Prairie and Frank participated in the many phases of the 1910 United Brethren Church restoration, which now houses the North Clark County Museum. He and Roberta are charter members and have been active there for 25 years.

Frank served as museum board president, building chairman and project manager at different times during the restoration. He and Roberta purchased the Wise house next to the church and made it a rental. Later he built a barn on the property to hold old horse-drawn equipment, farm implements and a blacksmith shop.

Active in the local North County community, Frank was a 50-year member of the Lions Club, the Volcano A's, and Farm Forestry membership. He rarely missed the Amboy Territorial Days parade, usually showing a square dance float or his two 1930 Model A's.

Frank lived on his grandparent's property until his death on June 28, last year. His wife and two sons survive him. He died quietly in the house he grew up in, close to the tools his hands knew so well and the cars he'd restored.

Howard Gingold

1930-2022

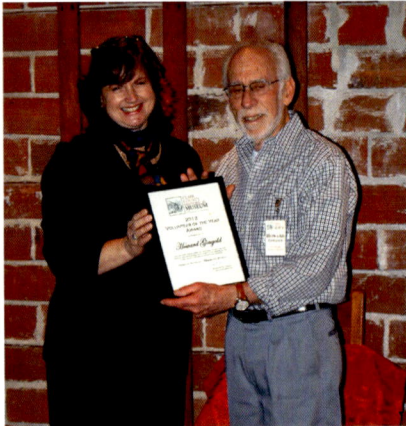

Howard Gingold   (Source: The Columbian)

After a distinguished career as a writer, producer, journalist and press secretary, Howard Gingold spent eight years of his retirement as the volunteer editor of Clark County History. He enjoyed telling stories and cast a new eye on Southwest Washington history, asking contributors to the publication to tell the story behind the story. His professional background and storytelling expertise made the publication livelier and more interesting for readers. The Clark County Historical Society awarded him its 2013 Volunteer of the Year award for his effort.

A native Los Angeleno, Howard studied journalism at the University of California, Berkley. A graduate school friend, Peter Noyes, called him "an excellent reporter who knew all the basics and reported accurately without bias or emotion." The two friends worked together at KNXT (CBS) to help produce the first-ever hour-long television news broadcast in the U.S.

Later, Howard became an on-air reporter and then Sacramento Bureau Chief for that media outlet. Before CBS, he was a reporter for the LA Times. After CBS, Howard worked as secretary to the Speaker of the California State Assembly and afterword moved to freelancing writer/producer of documentary television programs until his 2004 retirement.

He married Fayma Goldman in 2013, who, along with his two sons survive him. Fayma spent many hours volunteering and the historical museum and asked the director how her husband might get involved. From 2006 to 2014, he spent hours helping writers polish their stories and cleaning them up for publication.

Although may say Howard was witty, kind, caring and smart, the word most often attributed to him was gentleman, one who impacted the lives of others positively.

Janet Debra (Durgan) Ritter

1942-2022

Janet Ritter   (Source: Gene Ritter)

In 1853, Janet Debra (Durgan) Ritter's Durgan ancestors arrived in Clark County, the year the Washington Territory was formed. She lived her entire life within the county's borders except for a single year. She was educated at Providence Academy and Fort Vancouver High School, graduating in 1960. She attended Clark College.

Janet and her future husband, Gene Ritter, went waterskiing at Yale Reservoir in 1962 and married the following summer, connecting two families with a long history in the county. In celebration, they spent the final two days of their honeymoon waterskiing at the reservoir again. The couple had two children, one boy, Jeff and a girl, Susan. Jeff lives in Napa, California, while Susan lives in Hazel Dell, a short drive to her parents' home on Whipple Creek.

While Gene provided for the family by working in real estate, Janet ran their home turning it into a cozy place for her family. She was always available to transport and partake in her children's school activities. Once her two children were grown, Janet went back to work. She learned to use the computer and helped in her husband's real estate appraisal business, working side by side with him until they both retired in 2007.

Janet also sought out ways to assist other women. She was a lifetime member of the Clark County Historical Society, Daughters of the Pioneers, and in later life, joined PEO Chapter HL, an organization helping women of all ages achieve their educational goals.

Janet enjoyed her extended family and regularly hosted holiday dinners and gatherings, finding as many as 20 family members surrounding her dining room table. She spent her free time tending to her garden, planting flowers around her home, birdwatching and boating. She died on her favorite holiday Christmas.

Karen Wheeler Washabaugh

1948-2022

Karen and William Wheeler at their wedding ceremony.

Karen Washabaugh Wheeler was known as a dynamo of energy, an organizer, mentor, encourager, advocate and doer. She was also a competitive pistol target shooter and private pilot.

Karen worked as the visitor services coordinator at the Clark County Historical Museum for several years. Later she headed the museum's outreach efforts using digital and printed newsletters while managing the museum's research library. Karen was a museum team member working on annual events like the Harvest Fun Day and the Women's Tea. She supported the museum's administrative needs and worked closely with the executive director. She retired in 2014 while holding the interim executive director position.

The Washington Museum Association awarded Karen the Volunteer Contribution Award for her work on behalf of the museum, noting her contributions in support of creating an economic impact survey for the state group.

Her first husband was a United States Marine, and she became active in the Marine Corps League Auxiliary, holding leadership positions at the local, state and national levels. She was national president for two terms and volunteered with the Veterans Administration and other veteran service organizations.

As a member of Columbia Presbyterian Church, she held several roles, including choir member, Bible teacher and co-moderator of the Pastor Nominating Committee. She was even ordained as a deacon.

Her parents preceded Karen in death and her husband, Jerry Washabaugh. She is survived by her husband of six years, William Wheeler, and stepsons, Jess and Jay Washabaugh.

Born in Riverside, California Jan. 5, 1948, Karen was the only child of Jacob and Leatrice Yonker. She graduated from Corning High School, then completed a bachelor's degree from Chico State College and an MBA from Seattle International University. Karen worked as a computer programmer and in information technology for several organizations in Nevada, Seattle, and Vancouver. This detailed work helped to contribute to other roles she undertook.

Officers, Trustees, & Museum Staff

Pioneer & Life Members

Daughters of Pioneers Chapter 19
Barbara & John Barker
Caren L. Carlson
Larry & Jane Germann
Gill & Virginia Kleweno
Duane & Peggy Lansverk
James H. Malinowski
Robert Mealey
Steven & Karen Nelson
Myrtle E. Schultz
Irma C. Bauer Watson
Ed Wiswall
Robert Henry Wiswall Jr.
Mr. & Mrs. Paul Aldinger
Mary Anderson
Howard Anderson
Dr. Donald & Rosemary Ashley
Larry & Joann Bair
Linda Bakke
Dr. & Mrs. George Barton
Dollie Beers
Leonard Benner
Dorothy A. Blair
Dale F. Bowlin
Betty Brock
Scott & Jody Campbell
Greg Cermak
Richard W. Colf
Bob & Linda Colf
H. L. Corwin
Don & Pat Davis
Elliot Davis
Rose Diment
Robert & Debra Durgan
William Durgan
Philip Durkee
Flory Eby
Charles D. Ellington
Franklin & Roberta Emerick
Ferris English
John & Peggy Erickson
Hal & Jean Firestone
Bruce & Diane Firstenburg
Donald Fish Jr.
Donald Fish Sr.
Roberta H. Foster
Judy & Thomas Frink
Mrs. W. E. Frost
Harry Grady
Ruth Ham
Lawrence T. Hammett
Bill & Marcia Hidden
Monte Hidden
W. R. & M. L. Katschke
Joanne S. Kendall
Dovy Landerholm
Leland & Christina Larsen
John & Dona Marshall
Joyce McBride
Jim & Kay McClaskey
Bea Moore
Evelyn Morrow
Mary M. Nichols-Palena

Lowell Norris
Busse Nutley
Joe Palena
Dorothy Person
Vernon & Jelene Peterson
Mildred Piontek
Rudy Podhora
Emma Powell
Lee & Sondra Powell
Landis Kelly Punteney
Kenneth Puttkamer
Mary Louise Ransom
Dale Read Jr.
George Reich
Eugene Ritter
Gene & Janet Durgan Ritter
Jack & Kay Ritter
Wayne Ritter
Alan & Marcella Schurman

Elmer Schurman
David & Cecilia Smith
Eva M. Smith Wingert
Fred Spurrell
Noralee Stanton
Donald Stimpton
Orville H. Stout
Minnie Stromgren
Del & Sharon Swanson
Rod Swanson
Laura Takasumi
Lorraine Thompson
Louise M. Tucker
Virginia R. Van Breemen
Bob & Helen Wiswall
Ethel Young
Mary Zimmerman
David Zine